through the year with Saint Teresa of Avila

a little daily wisdom

through the year with Saint Teresa of Avila

a little daily wisdom

Saint Teresa of Avila

Compiled and modernized by
Bernard Bangley

PARACLETE PRESS
BREWSTER, MASSACHUSETTS

2013 Second Printing
2011 First Printing

A Little Daily Wisdom: Through the Year with St. Teresa of Avila

Copyright © 2011 by Bernard Bangley

ISBN 978-1-55725-697-3

Library of Congress Cataloging-in-Publication Data

Teresa, of Avila, Saint, 1515-1582.
  [Selections. English. 2011]
  A little daily wisdom : through the year with Saint Teresa of Avila / compiled and modernized by Bernard Bangley.
    p. cm.
  ISBN 978-1-55725-697-3
  1. Devotional calendars--Catholic Church. 2. Catholic Church--Prayers and devotions.
I. Bangley, Bernard, 1935- II. Title.
  BX2179.T3E5 2011
  242'.2--dc22   2010040660

10 9 8 7 6 5 4 3 2

Published by Paraclete Press
Brewster, Massachusetts
www.paracletepress.com
Printed in the United States of America

introduction

St. Teresa of Avila's life and writing destroy every notion that there are two kinds of religious personalities: active and contemplative. The story of Mary and Martha recorded in Luke 10:38–42, so beloved by generations of Christians, tends to make us think that the two patterns of behavior are clear opposites and mutually exclusive. The Christian is either a Martha, busy with the dishes, or a Mary, conversing with Jesus. Such a simple distinction is simply not true—not even for Mary and Martha. Most of us combine the characteristics of both, emphasizing one or the other as circumstances dictate or allow. Teresa is an outstanding example of a thorough blending of both.

Baptized in 1515 in Avila, Spain, as Teresa Sánchez de Cepeda y Ahumada, she was one of ten children in an affluent family. People considered Teresa a beautiful girl with a pleasant disposition. Her mother, Beatriz, died when Teresa was a teenager. Her father turned her care over to Augustinian nuns in 1531. At the age of twenty-one, without her father's approval, she fulfilled a personal dream and became a Carmelite nun in her hometown.

As a nun Teresa influenced the history and practices of the Roman Catholic Church in significant ways. She led her Carmelite order toward a stricter observance and ultimately founded fourteen monasteries. Her spirit of reform reached out through the cooperation of her friend Juan de la Cruz, known to us as St. John of the Cross, to change the manner of living for male Carmelites. The reformers used the terms *calced* and *discalced* (with shoes or without, i.e., barefoot) to denote the difference of humility they had brought about in their religious communities, which followed Teresa's practice of poverty and renunciation.

Plagued with very poor health, Teresa somehow managed to attend to a multitude of administrative details. She directed the work of laborers the way a modern contractor hires and oversees employees. She dealt with royalty and with "city hall" diplomatically. She put in an exhausting day that began with worship at five in the morning and often kept her at her desk until well past midnight.

It is this same busy, creative, determined administrator who is also one of the greatest contemplative spirits in history. While signing contracts or confuting her critics, she was aware that she was living her life in the presence of God. Teresa would not have us understand that in a figurative sense. She had a personal experience of mystical union with God through a remarkable prayer life that dominated her existence. She died in 1582 at the age of sixty-seven. Pope Gregory XV canonized her in 1622, and in 1970 she became, with St. Catherine of Siena, the first female Doctor of the Church.

Teresa wrote enduring books on prayer and Christian living. Her work will always be in print in many languages, and new versions continue to appear. The present book is unique because it is the first attempt to give an interested reader a broad exposure to the vast expanse of Teresian literature. If all you read of Teresa are the several famous passages relating her mystical experiences, you will gain a distorted notion of her. By spending a few moments each day for a full year with this volume, you will gain a solid familiarity with every aspect of Teresa's life and thought. I have gently paraphrased selections from the entire collection of her work into contemporary English.

Sometimes Teresa's writing becomes difficult as she attempts to express the inexpressible. She knows *what* she wants to say, but she has trouble determining *how* to say it. She fills many pages with brief prayers and expressions of exasperation. Teresa says there are no words available to describe her rapturous experiences. She is correct, but she attempts it anyway. Paraphrasing these breathless passages into contemporary English presents a considerable challenge, with a risk of distorting her ideas. Using extreme care, in a few places I have compressed an entire page into a single sentence. But ultimately I hope that this volume will be a springboard for you to discover the pleasure of reading one of the complete editions of Teresa's works.

Some of Teresa's terminology may seem strange to today's reader. I have often translated her use of a word into more familiar terms, but for accuracy a few examples of her specific terms remain. Five such words require explanation:

- HIS MAJESTY: This is one of Teresa's favorite nicknames for God. It reflects her reverent perception of the royalty and power of the divine. As closely as she lived with God, her manner of expression never became too familiar. She always exhibits the utmost courtesy and respect. She knows God rules and trusts him to get things done.

- PERFECTION: Jesus said, "Be perfect, therefore, as your heavenly Father is perfect" (Matt. 5:48). Scholars tell us the Greek word for perfection used here is in the future tense, implying the moral obligation of a correct attitude rather than perfect conduct of life. Perfection is integrity in our relationship with God. Moral perfection is not something we can attain here on earth. Teresa is not talking about legalism or an abstract ideal. Perfection, for her, is wholeheartedly serving God. The more we love God and neighbor, the more perfect we become.

- RECOLLECTION: In our time, this word refers to memory. When someone says, "I recollect," it is a matter of recalling something almost forgotten. In classic Christian spirituality, recollection refers to a tranquil mind undisturbed by wandering thoughts. A prayer of recollection turns our vision inward, away from externalities. Teresa thinks of recollection as the entrance to the interior life and an indicator that one's soul is prepared to receive.

- VISITATOR: This term refers to a representative of the pope who formally visited and inquired about conditions in a religious community. Personal interviews with superiors and members uncovered both joys and concerns, opening a way for support and correction.

- WORLD: Teresa exhibits a fondness for the natural world, often making strong points by mentioning birds, insects, flowers, springs, and the like. When she makes disparaging comments about the "world" she is not thinking of God's creation. Her reference is to the secular as opposed to the religious. She is expressing a disdain for material possessions and the aggressive and immoral means people use to obtain them.

I have selected and arranged material from Teresa's writings with no attempt at chronological order. Her style of writing is naturally conversational. Please keep in mind throughout this book that the liveliness in these pages is not the result of my translation.

The works included are described below, with my abbreviated title that identifies the source of each individual entry.

- AUTOBIOGRAPHY: Teresa penned the story of her life under orders to do so, directed by her confessor, sometime before 1567. The task was an unwelcomed chore during the shaky times of the Spanish Inquisition. She understood that some of her comments could cause her trouble. She never sought this kind of exposure for her personal struggle with God and the world. Somehow, she managed to avoid the pitfalls while delivering a rare record of spiritual progress. In her attempt to preserve her anonymity, Teresa never referred to herself by name (she typically used other identifiers such as "someone I know") and asked her confessor to respect her personal privacy if he decided to publish the work. Cited as LIFE.

- THE WAY OF PERFECTION: A practical guide to serious prayer by one who has practiced it, Teresa's most easily read book contains down-to-earth instruction for discovering a personal experience of the divine. This book was also written before 1567. Cited as WAY.

- THE INTERIOR CASTLE: Teresa's classic masterpiece develops in an orderly manner through seven stages, or levels. This is the ultimate guidebook for a contemplative life, written in 1577. Because her sequence of thought is important, I have confined most of my selections from this work to the autumn months, with a sprinkling of her digressive comments scattered throughout the year. Cited as CASTLE.

- THE BOOK OF FOUNDATIONS, 1573: Written to enlarge the story Teresa reports in her autobiography, including the history of the monasteries she had founded. Rather than provide only dry details, she fills it with spiritual advice, anecdotes, and practical lessons. Cited as FOUNDATIONS.

- THE CONSTITUTIONS, 1563: Whereas Teresa's other writings reveal a remarkable ability to nurture spirituality in a world filled with distractions and conflict, this work is an example of her administrative skills. She understands human nature and knows how to make reasonable rules to govern life together. Cited as CONSTITUTIONS.

- ON MAKING THE VISITATION, 1576: A brief treatise instructing papal "visitators" how to turn a formal routine into something valuable for each religious community. As usual, Teresa displays common sense and profound insight into the dynamics of convent life. Cited as VISITATION.

- LETTERS: Teresa wrote thousands of letters, often staying up until the wee hours of the morning. Those who respected the value of her correspondence collected more than 400 letters and fragments. Some are simply business but most communicate with friends conversationally and many contain spiritual insight. Teresa had to be circumspect when preparing books for publication because she knew her superiors would need to review and approve them. She is far more relaxed in her correspondence. Many rarely seen examples of her one-on-one spiritual instruction are included in this book. In her letters we can also discover that Teresa was as subject to ecclesiastical politics and personal power struggles as are modern church leaders. Many of her contemporaries did not treat her as a saint. Cited as LETTER TO [PERSON, YEAR].

- POETRY: Examples of Teresa's poetry are also presented here. Although not as talented a poet as her spiritual partner, John of the Cross, Teresa wrote charming poems to share with her friends and acquaintances. She even heard nuns set some of her lines to music. Cited as [TITLE OF POEM].

Teresa was a "people person," with an unusually large number of friends, correspondents, and business acquaintances. Some of these individuals interacted dramatically with Teresa and with one another. The people most central to her life and correspondence are briefly described below.

- JUAN DE LA CRUZ, known more widely as St. John of the Cross: Author of *Ascent of Mount Carmel, Dark Night of the Soul,* and *Spiritual Canticle*, a gifted Spanish poet, and the first male discalced Carmelite. Jailed and punished because of his efforts at religious reform, Juan worked closely with Teresa. Together they produced the apex of Spanish mystical literature.

- JERÓNIMO GRACIÁN: A discalced Carmelite friar considered by Teresa to be one of the best. Unusually well educated before becoming a priest, Gracián became acquainted with Teresa through her *Constitutions.* They met in 1575 and immediately became spiritual allies; she often addressed him as "my padre." Extremely helpful in Teresa's work, he suffered with her through tough and dangerous times, spending two agonizing years chained in a dark dungeon.

- LORENZO DE CEPEDA: Teresa's closest brother, who supported her financially and ultimately sought her spiritual direction. At nineteen he received serious wounds while fighting for Charles V in the Americas. In his final years he lived an almost monastic life on a farm near Avila.

- JUANA DE AHUMADA: Teresa's youngest sister. When their father died, Teresa assumed care of Juana for nine years.

- MARÍA BAUTISTA: Teresa's cousin and close friend who became the prioress of the monastery founded at Valladolid.

- BALTASAR ALVAREZ: Teresa's confessor when he was a newly ordained young priest. Teresa was beginning to have mystical experiences that confused Alvarez. She clearly perceived his discomfort. He lacked political connections and offered little assistance with her church and community conflicts. Still, she considered him a dear friend.

- TEUTONIO DE BRAGANZA: A Jesuit priest who quit after a disagreement with the founder of the Jesuits, St. Ignatius of Loyola. The son of the Duke of Braganza, he printed Teresa's *Way of Perfection* at his own expense.

- ISABEL DE JESÚS: Younger sister of Jerónimo Gracián, who entered the convent at Toledo when she was seven years old and became a nun at the age of sixteen. Teresa spoke of her affectionately and often. Blind during the final eighteen years of her life, Isabel lived until she was seventy-one.

a little daily wisdom

"We pray, not for our own pleasure and entertainment, but to find the strength to serve God."

—St. Teresa of Avila

january

1

At the beginning of the spiritual life it is a common temptation for us to want everyone else to be extremely spiritual. It is not wrong to want this, but it may not be right to try to make it happen. If we do, it is essential that we exercise discretion and give no impression that we are setting ourselves up as great teachers.

I discovered this for myself. When I attempted to induce others to pray, they would listen to what I had to say. When they then observed that I, the great practitioner of prayer, lacked certain virtues this would lead them astray. My actions were not compatible with my words. Across many years only three individuals have gained anything of value from what I have said to them.

We are also tempted to allow the sins and failings of others to distress us. We try to fix things. This excites us so much that it keeps us from praying. Worst of all, we trick ourselves into believing we are doing the Lord's work.

Try to focus on the best in others and the worst in ourselves. This will blind us to their defects. Eventually, we may even think of them as better than ourselves.

—LIFE

january 2

·

This is my early method of prayer. In the beginning I could not reflect expansively with my mind. I tried to imagine Christ within me. I had many simple thoughts of this kind.

The scene of Christ praying in the Garden of Gethsemane brought me much comfort. I tried to be his companion there. I attempted to imagine his sweat and agony in that place. I wanted to wipe the sweat from his brow, but I never allowed myself to do it. My sins seemed so serious to me.

I stayed with Christ in the garden as long as I could, but many distractions tormented me.

—LIFE

january 3
·

God does not put all of us on the same road. If you think you are on the lowest path of all, you may actually be on the highest in the Lord's view.

For me, contemplation and meditation are important. But these are God's gifts to me and are not necessary for salvation. It is not something God demands of us.

Don't be discouraged, then, and stop praying or participating in the community of faith. The Lord is not in a hurry. He gives to others now. He will give to you later.
—Way

january 4
·

Personally, I endured fourteen years without ever meditating satisfactorily unless I was reading something. I am not alone in this. Many Christians can't meditate even when they are reading. The best they can do is recite vocal prayers. Some have a problem with a short attention span. Unable to concentrate, they restlessly try to focus on God while fending off a thousand silly thoughts about religion.

I know a very old woman who is living an excellent life. I wish I were more like her. She is a penitent and a great servant of God. For years she has been praying the classic prayers aloud. Mental prayer is impossible for her. Many people are like this. This does not make them second-class Christians. Ultimately, many such people think they must be at fault. They think they are backward or handicapped.

Those God calls to an active ministry should not murmur against others who are absorbed in prayer. It is all in the same package. Whether your specialty is meditation and prayer or caring for the sick or sweeping floors in service to Christ, what should it matter? We are to do our best at whatever we do.

—WAY

january 5
·

Moaning and complaining when we have a little ailment is a sign of imperfection. If the sickness is bearable, don't talk about it. If the illness is serious, it will talk about itself with a distinctive kind of moaning.

If you are really sick, say so and take your medicine. If you have a minor ailment, which comes and goes, don't make a habit of talking about it all the time. Our bodies have one fault: the more we cater to them, the more things they want.

Learn to suffer a little for the love of God without needing to tell everyone about it. Keep your minor ailments a secret between you and God because talking about them does nothing at all to mitigate them.

Serious illness is another matter. I am thinking now about ordinary ailments, which you may have, but they are slight. With those, you can keep going. There is no need to bother everyone else.

Consider the holy hermits of past days. They endured tremendous sufferings in solitude. They were cold, hungry, and exposed to desert sun. They had no one to complain to except God. Do you think they were iron men? They were not. They were as frail as we are. When we start to subjugate these bodies of ours, they give us much less trouble. Our bodies mock us—now let's mock our bodies.

This is not a trifling matter. God will help us gain mastery of our flesh.

—WAY

january 6

Someone asked me to pray for him, but he did not need to ask, because I had already determined to pray. I went to my usual place for private prayer and began to speak foolishly with the Lord, as I often do when I am not sure what to say. That's when love is speaking, lifting me up to the point that I can't recognize any separation between my soul and God. When love understands it is in the presence of God, the soul loses self-consciousness and speaks absurdities.

I remember a time when I pleaded with God to commit me fully to his service. In my prayer I said I was not satisfied with simply thinking of God as good—I wanted to think of him as *very* good. I said to His Majesty, "Lord, please do not deny me this favor. Notice how this individual is qualified to be your friend."

O goodness and great humanity of God! You don't regard the language, but the desire and the determination behind such words. How can you put up with anyone as bold as I have been? May you be blessed forever.

—Life

january 7

I am sorry to read about the great difficulties you have experienced, my daughter, and that you must continue to endure so much important and necessary business. I know what that's like. Still, I don't believe you would feel any better if you could find the undisturbed quiet you desire, and it could actually make you feel worse. I am absolutely sure of this because I am familiar with your disposition. I accept the fact that you will find it necessary to undergo distress. Such trials are the experiences that produce saints. The longing you have for solitude is better than the possession of it.
—Letter to María Bautista, 1574

january 8

God, you are infinitely good. You have made me your friend. You waited patiently and favored me. You waited for me to adjust to your nature while enduring my nature. In a moment of repentance, you forget my offensiveness.

I am not able to understand, my Creator, why everyone is not trying to become your special friend. Why do the wicked refuse to allow you to be with them a few hours a day? A thousand worldly cares and worries keep them away the same way such concerns hindered me.

—LIFE

january 9

·

When I enjoyed being with the Lord today, I made a bold complaint. I asked him, "Why, my God, do you keep me in this miserable life? Everything here gets in the way of my spiritual pleasure. I must eat, sleep, conduct business, and talk with everyone who needs my attention. I accept this great torment because of my love for you. But why do you hide from me when I finally find a little time to enjoy your presence? Is this a reflection of divine mercy? I don't understand how your love for me can allow this. I am never out of your sight. You are always with me, and there is no way I could ever hide from you."

Sometimes love makes me foolish. The Lord puts up with my nonsense. I praise such a good King! We would never dare to make remarks like this to earthly kings.

—LIFE

january 10

In combat, the standard-bearer is not armed. His exposure to danger is as great as the other soldiers, but it is not his job to fight. He will suffer as much as anyone else, but he cannot defend himself. He is carrying the flag and must not allow it to leave his hands even if the enemy is cutting him to pieces.

Christians need to hold the cross of Jesus high. It is our duty to suffer with Christ. This is a duty with high honor. Think about it! If the standard-bearer lets the flag fall, the battle will be lost. The other soldiers can retreat if they must, and no one will notice. They have no loss of honor. But everyone is looking at the flag for inspiration. It must hold its ground. This is a noble assignment. The king gives great honor to anyone who accepts it. It is a serious obligation.

The Lord knows us as we really are. He gives each of us work to do. He understands what is most appropriate for us, what will be helpful to him, and what will be good for others. Unless you fail to prepare yourself for your assignment, you can be sure it will be successful.

—WAY

january 11

Our prayer for those who give us light should be unceasing. With the storms that rage in the church today, what would we do without them?

If some clergy have gone bad, the good ones shine more brilliantly.

May it please the Lord to keep those who lead the church under his care. God help them that they might help us.

—LIFE

january 12

•

I am not surprised to read that you are dissatisfied with yourself. You should not be astonished that you are experiencing some cooling of your spiritual life, when you consider stressful travel and the demands for your time. When things settle down, your soul will also calm.

My own health has improved. I was seriously ill for about two months, and the sickness degraded my interior life. It was almost as though I were not present. Inside, improvement has already started; outside, I have common ailments.

I am getting along well with Padre Santander, but not very well with the Franciscan friars. We purchased a house that is exactly what we want, but it is close to their house, and they have started legal proceedings against us. I can't imagine how all of this will end.

—LETTER TO TEUTONIO DE BRAGANZA, 1574

january 13

A void statements like these: "I was right." "They did not have the right to do this to me." God deliver us from such false notions of what is right! Do you think it was right for Jesus to suffer all those insults? Did the people who did those bad things to a good man have the right to do so? Why do we think we should only bear crosses we think we have the right to expect?

Do you think you have to put up with so much now that you have the right not to bear any more? How does the question of rightness even enter this discussion? It has nothing to do with it.

When we are offended and hurt, there is nothing to complain about. We can share the dishonor with Christ. Consider yourself fortunate to have such an opportunity, and you will lack honor neither in this life nor in the next.

—WAY

january 14

O my Lord, you seem determined to save me. I pray this may happen.

But since you have granted me so many favors, doesn't it seem reasonable that it would be a good thing (not for my benefit, but for your honor) if the inn where you continually dwell did not get so dirty?

—LIFE

january 15

S ome people believe that devotion will slip away from them if they relax a little. I believe recreation is good for the soul. If we relax a while, we will be stronger when we return to prayer.

Do not spend all of your time in one method of prayer even if you have found an excellent method of prayer that you really enjoy. You may need a kind of Sunday. I mean a time of rest from your spiritual labor.

You might think that you will lose something if you stop working at prayer. My view is that your loss would be gain. Try to imagine yourself in the presence of Christ. Talk with him. Delight in him. There is no need to weary yourself by composing great speeches to him.

There is a time for one thing and a time for another. The soul can become weary of eating the same food over and over again. Remember that there is a great variety of food that is wholesome and nutritious. If your spiritual palate becomes familiar with their various tastes, they will sustain the life of your soul, bringing many benefits.

—LIFE

january 16

Beginning my life as a nun brought many changes. The new diet affected my health. While I was extraordinarily pleased to be a nun, this was not enough to make me well. I frequently fainted and had chest pain. My sickness alarmed anyone who saw it happen. In fact, my first year at the Incarnation convent brought innumerable puzzling illnesses. The only good thing about my ailments is that I did not have much energy remaining to offend God.

As the year progressed I was unconscious more than I was awake. The seriousness of my maladies made my father seek a cure, since community doctors had run out of treatments. My father made arrangements to deliver me to a healer who lived in my sister's village and had a reputation for success with difficult cases.

Since the Incarnation was not cloistered, the senior nun, Juana, accompanied me to María's house where I could stay during the course of treatment. I endured three months of extraordinary procedures that nearly killed me. I am amazed that I survived. My health suffered permanent damage because of the beating I took from these alleged "cures."

—Life

january 17

•

Your letter arrived more than two months ago. I should have answered quickly, but I delayed while waiting for things to calm down. The reformed friars and nuns have experienced great trials. By holding off, I had hoped to send you some good news, but things have become worse every day.

Have faith that God will certainly hear the prayers made by souls who want nothing more than to serve God. This is my constant prayer, and it is the prayer of all your servants in these monasteries. Not a day goes by that I do not find souls who put me to shame. The Lord himself must be selecting them and directing them to our houses from far away.

—LETTER TO TEUTONIO DE BRAGANZA, 1578

january 18

Do not take my comments as infallible. For a subject as complex as prayer, that would be a foolish notion. There are many paths along this spiritual way and I may manage to write a few helpful things about some of them, but if you do not walk the same path I am walking you may not understand what I am saying. If my words do not help anyone, the Lord will accept my desire to help.

Some consider mental prayer the perfect prayer. They try to keep their mind focused on God. This requires tremendous effort and they are satisfied that it makes them spiritual. If life requires other good work of them, they become distressed and think everything is lost. No doubt it is a special privilege from the Lord to be able to meditate continuously. There is nothing wrong with trying to sustain this kind of prayer. What we need to remember, though, is that not everyone is capable of doing this. But all souls have the capacity for love. The soul is not the mind any more than thinking controls the will. Above all, spiritual progress does not lie in thinking much, but in loving much.

—FOUNDATIONS

january 19

•

My hair stood on end when I received Communion. The Lord frequently wants me to see his astonishing splendor in the bread. The experience left me limp.

O my Lord! If you did not subdue your radiance, none of us could even approach Communion. May all angels and creatures sing your praises.

You give yourself in proportion to our weakness in order to prevent terrifying us. You reveal yourself a little at a time. I am astonished that I can perceive something as extraordinary as your majesty in a piece of bread.

—LIFE

january 20

We once had a deep well with very bad water that would not flow. I asked some workmen to dig us a new well, but they laughed at me for wanting to throw money away. I asked the sisters for their opinion. One of them thought we should try, reasoning that without a functioning well we would have to pay someone to bring us water. It would be cheaper for God to give us a well on the grounds, and he would certainly do so. She convinced me because she spoke with so much faith and conviction. Going against the opinion of the foreman who knew everything about wells and water, I told him to dig. The Lord was pleased that we were able to construct a pipeline that now provides all the water we need.

I am not saying this is a miracle, although I could tell you some other things. The point is: what faith these sisters have!

—FOUNDATIONS

january 21

It is dangerous to review the years during which we have prayed. We may come to think that we have won some prize by serving God. It's not that our service doesn't have any merit or reward. The problem is that if a spiritual person dwells on these things it may not be possible to reach the summit of spirituality.

The more we serve God, the more we are in debt to him. It is as though God gives us thousands of dollars and we pay back a few pennies. For the love of God, let's leave all this to him. Sometimes he will give the same pay to the last workers as to the first.

—LIFE

january 22

It is possible, while you are praying the Lord's Prayer (or some other vocal prayer), that the Lord will give you *perfect contemplation*. This turns prayer into an actual conversation with God, working beyond understanding. Words become unimportant. Anyone who experiences this will know that the divine Master is doing the teaching without the sound of words.

The soul is aroused to love without understanding how it loves. It comprehends how distinctly different this moment is from all others. This is an unearned gift of God. Such an experience is not the equivalent of mental prayer, which is silently thinking about what we are saying and to whom we are saying it. Don't think of it as something esoteric with an unusual name. Don't let the technical term for it frighten you away. In regular prayer we are taking the lead with God's help. In perfect contemplation, God does everything. It is not easy to explain.

—WAY

january 23

•

M y desire is to describe clearly matters related to prayer. This will be very difficult for the uninitiated to understand.

It is best for a soul not to attempt to rise by its own efforts. If the well is dry we are not able to put water into it. Pay attention to this. If the soul tries to go forward it may actually go backward. Also, the foundation for prayer is humility. The nearer we come to God, the more humility we need. There is a kind of pride that makes us want to be more spiritual. God is already doing more for us than we deserve.

When I say that people should not attempt to rise unless God lifts them up, I am using spiritual language. Some will understand me. If you can't understand what I am saying, I don't know another way to explain it.

—LIFE

january 24

•

As night was coming on, we approached the town of Arévalo. We were fatigued because of our poor provisions for travel. A priest we knew came out to meet us. He had arranged lodging for us in the home of some devout women. In private, he informed me the house we had rented was near an Augustinian monastery that did not want us there and was certain to bring a lawsuit. With the courage God gives, small things like this do not matter. I told him to keep quiet about it in order to spare my companions grief.

—FOUNDATIONS

january 25

I did not have the money for necessary work on our monastery even though it was a small one with no more than fifteen nuns. I simply trusted God. If God wants it done, God will provide. I foolishly bargained with the laborers I could not afford.

Now it is clear that His Majesty has encouraged you to help us pay for it! And the remarkable thing is that the forty pesos you sent are precisely what I owed.

Our small house is plain, but we have a field with gorgeous views. That's enough to satisfy us.

—LETTER TO LORENZO DE CEPEDA, 1561

Worrying about financial support seems to me a worldly waste of energy. Regardless of how much you fret about it, you will not change any giver's mind or make anyone eager to contribute alms. Leave these concerns to God who can move everyone, who is Lord of all money and those who possess it. If we do not fail God, God will not fail us. If it seems that we lack support, it will do us good.

Those who give too much attention to money eventually will allow this bad habit to prompt them to ask another for something they don't need. They may possibly ask alms from someone who actually needs it more. That person would gain rather than lose by giving it to us, but we would be much worse off when we receive it.

I beg you, for the love of God, as though I were begging alms for you, do not allow these things to occupy your thoughts. We will find blessings in holy poverty.

—WAY

january 27

·

Honor and money go together. The one who desires honor never hates money, but the one who hates money has little regard for honor. The world rarely honors an honorable poor person. Instead, it despises him. True poverty bears a different kind of honor that is never objectionable. I'm thinking of poverty we welcome for God's sake. In my experience, I have learned that if you have no need of anyone you will have many friends.

I have read a lot about this virtue we name "poverty" that is beyond my understanding and ability to express. I would only make things worse if I were to eulogize it now, so I'll say no more about it.

—WAY

Your distress comes as no surprise to me. I knew you would have some troubled times, because you do not have an outgoing personality.

What you are attempting is for the Lord's service, so please don't give up. Discuss the details with someone. Don't fret about them.

I am also concerned for your health. My own health has been poor recently. It would be worse except for the comfort your house brings me. My pain increased so much that when I got to Toledo I needed two bleedings. I needed to remain still in bed because great pain moved from my shoulders up to the back of my head. I ardently pray for you. I am better now, though still weak.

The priest from Malagón came with me and I owe him many thanks.

—LETTER TO LUISA DE LA CERDA, 1568

january 29
.

It delighted me to think of my soul as a garden in which my Lord walked. He turned a nasty dung heap into a beautiful flower garden.

Now I need to be careful not to pull up the plants he introduced, thus allowing the garden to return to waste.
—LIFE

january 30
.

Here in Valladolid some of the most influential residents express strong opposition to my work. For the moment, we have smoothed this over. Never think that you will give the Lord only what you think is enough. Much more will be required. His Majesty demonstrates his pleasure in our good works by asking for more. Giving money is a trifling act because it doesn't cause great pain. When they throw stones at you and the rest of us who are busy with this project (the way they almost did in Avila when we founded St. Joseph's) our labor will thrive. I am certain that the monastery, and those of us who suffer, will lose nothing, and that much good will result. Let the Lord take control and do things as he pleases. Don't be sad. May God be blessed, because if we do not fail God, God will not fail us.

—LETTER TO ALONSO RAMIREZ, 1569

january 31

•

Have you noticed how God is at work in Lorenzo de Cepeda? Lorenzo is paying more attention to his children's salvation than to making a lot of money. O Jesus, I owe you so much! How small is my service to you! Nothing brings me greater happiness than seeing the brothers I love inspired to want the best.

Remember how I told you to leave everything in God's hands, assuring you that he would take care of it all. I repeat this advice. Turn everything over to God. God will always do what is best for us.

Thinking about the joy that will be yours brings me pleasure. May God give us lasting joy. We cannot trust the pleasures of this life.

—Letter to Juana de Ahumada, 1569

february

I loved my family, and my father's disapproval of my decision to become a nun weighed heavily upon me. I felt as if I were dying on the day my brother Antonio and I took a trip to investigate the possibilities of entering the religious life.

I needed God's help and I got it. The Lord helped me to fight with myself. I found my calling, and I accepted the habit of a nun. No one could imagine the personal struggle I was having at that time. They thought my taking vows resulted from untainted desire.

This new life brought me great joy that has never diminished. Everything about the religious life was a pleasure, even sweeping the floors. Formerly, I wasted so much time grooming and dressing myself. Realizing I was now free of these things brought a wave of happiness.

—LIFE

february 2

·

When I repeat the Lord's Prayer, my love causes me to desire to understand who this Father is and who this Master is who taught us the prayer.

You are wrong if you think you already know who he is.

We should think of him every time we say his prayer. Human frailty may interfere with this. When we are sick or our heads are tired, no matter how hard we try we may not be able to concentrate. If we are going through stormy times we may be too distressed to pay attention to what we are saying. As hard as we try, we just can't do it.

Imagine that Jesus taught this prayer to each one of us individually and that he continues to explain it to us. He is always close enough to hear us. To pray the Lord's Prayer well, there is one thing you need to do. Stay near the side of the Master who taught it to you.

"Ah!" you say. "This is meditation. I am not able to meditate. I have no desire to meditate. I am content to pray this prayer out loud." Maybe you are one of those impatient people who don't like to be bothered. Yes, it is a little troublesome to begin to consider Jesus when you pray the

Lord's Prayer, until it becomes habitual. You are right. This step turns vocal prayer into mental prayer. In my view, it is faithful vocal prayer. We need to think about who is listening.

—WAY

february 3

•

May you be blessed forever, Lord God! Although I abandoned you, you did not abandon me. You held out your hand to me. I refused it. I did not attempt to understand why you kept calling me.

As sins increased I lost my taste for virtue. Goodness left me because I left you. You warned me in many ways with concern and pity. I gave you no attention.

O Lord of my soul! How can I applaud the good will you showed me during those years? When I offended you the most, you prepared me with an extraordinary repentance. You knew exactly what would be the most distressing thing for me. You punished my sins with wonderful gifts.

I had many friends who helped me fall. No one helped me up. It is surprising that I did not remain down. I praise the mercy of God. He alone extended his hand to me.

May God be forever blessed for putting up with me for so long. Amen.

—LIFE

february 4

·

J esus be with you. I praise God that after writing a half-dozen or more necessary business letters, I can take a little break and write these lines to let you know how appreciative I am of your letters to me.

Don't imagine that it is a waste of your time to write me.

The only thing I request is that you stop telling me you are getting old. I am dismayed. Is there something more secure in being young?

May God allow you to remain on earth while I am alive.

And after I die, in order to prevent being in heaven without you, I will ask the Lord to quickly bring you there!

—LETTER TO FRANCISCO DE SALCEDO, 1568

february 5

When I entered Our Lady of Grace I met a nun who had conversations about the sacred with me. She told me about the great treasure the Lord shares with those who turn aside for him. Her friendship corrected the bad habits I was forming. I began to think of God again, and my interest in eternal things returned.

I envied any nun I saw who would weep as she prayed. It bothered me that I could read every verse about the crucifixion of Christ and never wring out a single holy tear.

—LIFE

february 6

Don't fatigue yourself with too much thinking and meditation. Always praise the Lord and desire everyone else to do the same. This is the greatest result of occupying your soul with God.

Also, you and I need to find out how to repay a little of what we owe His Majesty. May he send us a lot of suffering,

even if it comes in the form of fleas, hobgoblins, and traveling.
—LETTER TO ANTONIO GAYTÁN, 1574

february 7

My Uncle Pedro asked me to visit him and read to him. The only subject of his reading and conversation was God's glory and the world's emptiness. I had no interest in his books, but I tried to make him happy by feigning pleasure.

O God, you were preparing my soul in small increments. You constrained me until I could constrain myself.

I was with Uncle Pedro for only a few days, but exposure to the instruction in his home took hold of me. God's Word mixed with his positive companionship, reminding me of my childhood conclusions that this world is passing and that nothing is permanent.
—LIFE

february 8

·

In spite of the risks you face because of your youth, wealth, and independence, the Holy Spirit has enlightened you to discard them all. I also know that you understand the value of penance, enclosure, and poverty—things that ordinarily repel others.

You have quickly persuaded me that you have the capacity to be one of Our Lady's daughters. Padre Juan de León told me all about you. You have the makings of a saint.

May the Lord reward you for your large amount of alms. You must be satisfied that you are doing what the Lord advises by giving yourself to him and what you have to the poor, because you love him. Because you have received so much, you could not have fulfilled your commitment with less. You are doing as much as you can, and you will receive much in return.

You have already read our constitution and rule. If you continue in your decision, you may enter whenever you wish, and you may move into whichever of our houses you prefer. I hope you will come here with me, because I want to know you personally as a friend. Our Lord will lead you in everything for his greater service and glory. Amen.

—Letter to Isabel de Jimena, 1570

february 9

My Uncle Pedro gave me a copy of *The Third Spiritual Alphabet* by Francisco de Osuna. The author discusses the Prayer of Recollection. I had begun to realize how much damage my great interest in romance novels was doing to my soul. A great appreciation for spiritual books was growing in me. I knew nothing about contemplative prayer or anything about recollecting my senses and thoughts. This book told me precisely what to do, and I was excited.

I began to work seriously at contemplation. God finally had given me the gift of tears. I spent hours alone, reading and weeping. I often went to confession. I did the best I could with Francisco de Osuna's book to guide me. None of the spiritual masters understood me. I looked for one for twenty years. Without any kind of guidance, I often missed the way. If only someone could have kept me from offending God!

—Life

february 10

·

Beware of thinking about your seniority. May God help us to avoid thoughts such as these: "But I have been here the longest." "I have worked harder." "Someone else is being favored."

If these kinds of thoughts come into your head, be quick to hold them in check. If you allow yourself to dwell on these ideas or include them in your conversation, they will spread like a plague. In church they will result in serious problems.

God deliver us from Christian servants who care about their own honor. Think how little they gain from it. The very act of wanting others to honor us robs us of honor. There is no poison in the world more fatal to a life of faith.

You may reply that these are little human foibles that we don't need to worry about. I tell you it is not a trifling matter. In churches these poisonous thoughts spread like foam on water. This kind of sensitivity is extremely dangerous. There are many reasons why this is so. It may be rooted in some trivial thing, but it will grow.

—WAY

february 11

Suppose someone thinks it is an act of love to report an offense to you. She asks you how you can allow yourself to be insulted like this. The reporter assures you of her prayers because even a saint could not take more. But the devil is putting his poisonous words in another's mouth. You may be willing to bear the slight, but now egotism tempts you.

Our human nature is terribly weak. Even while we are protesting that there is nothing to make a fuss about, we imagine we are doing something good. We begin to feel sorry for ourselves. If others say they are sorry for us, that only makes it worse.

For the love of God, never show pity to another person for anything that has to do with imagined insults.

—WAY

february 12

•

I was tempted to think that I would never be able to survive the rigors of the religious life because I grew up in luxury and comfort. When I considered everything that Christ endured, I decided that I could accept some hardship for his sake. I don't know how much help I expected him to give me. I had never enjoyed good health, but now I suffered fever and dizziness.

My admiration for good books kept me going. St. Jerome's letters gave me the courage to tell my father I had decided to become a nun. Telling him was as great a moment for me as putting on the habit. Of course he did not approve my plan. No one was able to convince him it was a good idea for him to let me go. But he told me that I could do anything I wanted after his death.

When that time came I needed to act quickly. My desire would have faded if I had delayed.

—Life

february 13

Jesus. The Holy Spirit be with you. Bless God for everything.

The fact that you are suffering so many difficulties is clear evidence of your love for the Lord. When you patiently accept problems the way you are enduring them, you open the way for God to grant you even more favors.

A great blessing would be for you to start to grasp the futility of giving a lot of attention to a life that continually reminds us that it is perishing. Then we can begin to see how much we should cherish and seek the life that never ends.

—LETTER TO GUIOMAR PARDO TAVERA, 1571

february 14

Your problems blend with my own suffering. There is no need to ask the Lord to give us any more. Thank God for everything. He is already allowing you to sip from the chalice of illnesses.

I read that God's love is the recompense for trials. With a return so valuable, we welcome them. I urge you to respond to your difficulties in this spirit. These things will become history soon enough. Live your life detached from anything that does not last eternally.

My own health is good—praise God—compared with what I have come to expect. With so much work to do, I would collapse without better than ordinary health. I have many responsibilities that demand my attention both inside and outside the Incarnation in Avila. There is hardly enough time to write this message.

—LETTER TO LUISA DE LA CERDA, 1571

february 15

•

I am familiar with a quiet life in our houses. But in this place I live with pandemonium. Still, glory to God, I am at peace inside.

I have started to change the rules here, gradually taking away distractions from the nuns. They are surely good, virtuous women, but changing old habits is like dying. They seem to respect me, and they are trying to accept the new rules. With 130 nuns it is important to keep things orderly.

My thoughts return to our own monasteries, but since I am here under obedience I ask the Lord to keep me from failing in my duty. This is a Babylon that I accept as a favor from God. It does not disturb my soul, though my human nature is fatigued.

—LETTER TO LUISA DE LA CERDA, 1571

february 16

•

If secular society has little respect for God, how can we expect it to have any for us? Do we deserve better treatment than God? Have we done more for people than Jesus? What should we expect? Still, it is distressing to see so many souls on the way to hell. I wish there were not so many, yet more are being lost every day.

I laugh, but it saddens me when I hear the things for which people ask us to pray. They want us to pray that God will give them money. It would be better if they would ask

God to help them crush all worldly things beneath their feet. They mean well, and I respond to their requests because I think they are sincerely devout. But I don't think God ever listens to me when I pray for such things.

—WAY

february 17

L ord, you have arranged a delicate and extraordinarily heavy cross for anyone who reaches this spiritual state. I call it "delicate" because it pleases me and "heavy" because it is sometimes more than I can bear. Still, the only thing any soul would exchange it for is being with you. My soul remembers that it has been your poor servant.

If continuing to live presents me with more opportunities to serve you, then I desire an even heavier cross and I would not want to die until the end of the world. The only rest my soul can have is in rendering some small service to you.

While my soul doesn't understand its own desires, it fully understands it wants nothing other than God.

—LIFE

february 18

True humility lies in being satisfied with our responsibility. Do your assigned task with good cheer. Let others do their jobs. Some of us want to ask God for favors. Do you call *that* humility?

Spiritual progress has nothing to do with having the most answers to prayer, or with raptures, visions, and favors from the Lord. We won't know the value of those things until we die. What I have been describing is for right now.

—WAY

february 19

I would not hesitate to do anything the Beloved asks, regardless of its difficulty. Experience has taught me that when I accept a challenge for his sake, a gnawing doubt regarding my ability to perform will bless me. When the work is finished, the reward is high satisfaction. This is a reward we receive here and now rather than in heaven.

The only ones who can understand what I am saying are those who have also tasted these sweet pleasures. I have been through this many times.

Sometimes an assignment has far-reaching implications. In such cases, I will give you my best advice: If you are inspired to take on a worthy project, don't hesitate. Have no fear that you may not be able to accomplish it. Turn yourself over to God. Take yourself out of it. You need not be afraid you can't do the job. God can do all things.

—LIFE

february 20

I have been thinking of you, concerned that this bad weather could be detrimental to your health. Bless God. Eventually we will experience an eternity where there are no changes in weather.

The climate in this area has been a trial for me even though I was born here. Since I returned six months ago, I have not had six weeks of good health. The Lord understands my limitations and does my work for me.

I stay busy trying to take care of myself. Three weeks ago the recurring fever I experience combined with pain in my side and a seriously sore throat. The troubling thing is that I am too feeble to stir, except for Mass.

I am telling you all of this so that you will not criticize me for failing to write. From the moment I arrived here I have had to endure overwhelming weakness and illness. My responsibility for this house and the complex business of our other monasteries exhausts me. I am an example of St. Paul's teaching that we can do all things in God who provides the power. In spite of my many illnesses I am able to perform all my responsibilities. Sometimes I laugh with myself about it. Loneliness comes with my position. I have no friend here in whom I may confide. I must always be on my guard when I speak.

—LETTER TO MARÍA DE MENDOZA, 1572

february 21

•

Prayer of union with God produces spiritual tenderness. The soul desires to be consumed and is driven to weep—tears of joy rather than sadness. It becomes aware of the moisture of the tears but has no idea when they flowed. It is pleased that the same water that extinguishes fire can also increase its flames. This may seem contradictory, but it is the way it happens.

When my spiritual life was in its early stages this prayer of union was a brief experience. I drifted so far away from myself that I could not be sure if it was a dream or if this sensation of glory was really happening. The moisture of my tears, like a shower from heaven, assured me my experience was genuine.

A soul in this degree of prayer is overwhelmed with courage. It would take pleasure in being chopped into pieces for God. Prayer of union produces great resolve, grand promises, and fervent desire. There is no doubt about the vanity and worthlessness of earthly things. Prayer of union purifies and elevates the soul.

Deeper humility also comes. The soul understands it had absolutely nothing to do with the munificent and superb gift it is receiving and that it does not possess the ability to keep it. Its unworthiness is painfully clear because cobwebs cannot hide from a flood of sunlight.

—LIFE

february 22

A spiritual person once said, "I am not as astonished by the things done by a soul in mortal sin as I am by the things *not* done by it." May a merciful God spare us such great evil. This neglect is the thing we should fear. When you pray, beg God to deliver you from it.

I have learned two important lessons: first, be most concerned about offending God; second, let this be a mirror of humility, as we understand that any good we do has its source in God. Without God's help, we are powerless. Following any good behavior, turn your thoughts immediately to God and not to yourself.

—CASTLE

·

I have learned, through experience as well as reading, that an obedient soul receives much blessing. Through obedience, we advance in virtue and gain humility. Obedience prevents us from worrying about straying from the path to heaven.

We also gain a precious spiritual relaxation. Once we completely resign ourselves to the practice of holy obedience, surrendering our thoughts and not seeking any other opinion than our confessor or superior, the devil will stop harassing us. Our restless fidgeting, which makes us eager to do what we desire even if it is unreasonable, ceases.

—Foundations

february 24

In my youth some of our more secular cousins would visit our home. I wish my father had watched them more carefully. Looking back, I realize it is risky to expose children to negative influences during their moral development. Although these relatives were not depraved, they had a way of exciting wicked ideas in me.

We were all about the same age, but a few were slightly older. We were together a lot. I tried to amuse them with my comments, and I listened carefully when they reported their misadventures. My soul sank into an evil whirlpool.

My advice to parents is that they should be careful regarding their children's companions. Bad playmates are a risk. Youth naturally gravitate toward what is harmful rather than what is helpful. This was undoubtedly true for me.

My personal experience is proof that one person can destructively influence another's soul, especially when they are young. If you are a parent, pay attention to me and be careful.

—LIFE

february 25

•

God wanted me for himself. Even though I did not seek it, God protected me from great hazards. My secret affairs did not remain as secret as I thought. Less than three months into my youthful rebellion, my father began to notice the change in me. He sent me to Our Lady of Grace, an Augustinian convent in our area. There, young people could live in a sheltered environment while getting an education. This was a reasonable thing for me to do. My sister had married and my mother was dead. It was not proper for a girl to live alone without the oversight of a mature woman.

I had hidden my tracks so that no one could prove my childish misbehavior. I did not remember that nothing is secret to God.

O beloved Lord, we make serious mistakes when we neglect you. You would spare us so much suffering if we remained constantly aware of you. This would protect us, not from others, but from ourselves.

—LIFE

february 26

How do you excuse yourself for failing to mention how sick you are? This bothers me. You are misguided to be concerned about perfection when you should be spoiling yourself. Your health matters to us.

You are very much like me. I admit that I have never been even nearly perfect. Now I am old and tired and I think I have an excuse. You would be bothered if you saw me. My stomach has been unsettled, which makes the nuts you sent me a welcomed treat. I still had a few nuts left from last time, but these fresh ones are very good. You eat the ones you still have for love of me.

I received three packets of mail today and many yesterday. Because my confessor is at the grille and wants me to send this messenger off as soon as possible, I'm not able to write you a long letter.

—Letter to María Bautista, 1574

•

Be patient with me. I am writing about a subject of which I am ignorant. Foolishly, I pick up paper and pen without any notion of what to write or how to begin. I know it is important to anyone who is reading that I should explain interior experiences as clearly as possible.

We agree that prayer is worthwhile. Our constitutions require that we pray a number of hours a day, but no mention is made of how to pray or of the supernatural work of the Lord in the soul.

While God has shed light on some of the things I have written, I have not understood all of it myself. Writing about the intricate depths of prayer demands careful preparation in the earliest pages. I must put on paper the most commonly known elementary ideas.

—CASTLE

february 28

•

I plead with Sister Beatriz and Sister Margarita to behave as I have asked all nuns to do: forget past mistakes. Do not talk about such things with anyone other than our Lord or a confessor. When you speak, speak with simplicity and love, making no accusations. Focus on pleasing the Lord. There is no reason to give any more attention to what has happened.

The Lord frequently allows us to stumble because this develops our humility. When we recover, we do better next time, making advances in the service of our Lord. This is a pattern we can see in the lives of many saints. You are daughters and sisters of the Blessed Virgin. Try to love each other. Attempt to live as though nothing troubling ever happened.

—LETTER TO THE NUNS AT SEVILLE, 1580

•

Since you have surrendered happiness and relaxation in this life, the Lord will give you eternal happiness and rest. Eventually, you will see how much you have gained. Nothing in this world will ever tempt you to give it up.

We should not feel sorry for those who die. God has taken them out of this dangerous and unstable world. We weep for ourselves rather than for those who now benefit from a larger good.

—LETTER TO LUISA DE LA CERDA, 1571

march

I f your mind wanders during prayer, here is a technique that will certainly help: if you are a prayer beginner, there is no need now for subtle meditation with many mental conceptions of Jesus. Simply look at him.

If you are in trouble or sad, look at Jesus on his way to the Garden of Gethsemane. Imagine the struggle going on inside his soul. See him bending under the weight of the cross. Look at him persecuted, suffering, and deserted by his friends.

Let your prayer begin to take shape. "Lord, if you are willing to suffer such things for me, what am I suffering for you? Why should I complain? Let me imitate your way. I will suffer whatever I must and consider it a blessing. Where you go, I will go. We will suffer together."

Consider how much more difficult his troubles are than yours. As painful as your own struggles may be, they will become a source of comfort for you.

You ask me how you can possibly do this, protesting that Jesus is not physically present in the world today. Listen! Anyone can make the little effort it takes to look at the Lord within. You can do this without any risk and with very little bother. If you refuse to try this, it is not likely that you would have remained at the foot of the cross either.

—Way

march 2
•

I pray that the Lord will allow your behavior to match your outstanding reputation here. People continually praise you and refer to you as a saint. I praise the Lord that you have given them that kind of example. It results from suffering much hardship. The Lord uses the fire of love he places in your soul to ignite similar fire in others. Therefore, be of good courage. Remember our Lord's suffering during this season of the year. Life is short and we face only a brief trial here.

—Letter to Doña María de Mendoza, 1569

march 3

While I was at my sister's home receiving treatment for my mysterious illness, the Lord started blessing me with spiritual gifts. I was able to direct my soul in positive directions, but not with great skill. Francisco de Osuma's book regarding the Prayer of Recollection assured me that by now I should be right on target, but I was not able to achieve this degree of consciousness. I was concerned about making big mistakes.

The generosity of the Beloved led me to the Prayer of Quiet. On one occasion I even experienced the Prayer of Union. When these things happened I had no idea what was going on or how valuable they were. I would have gotten more out of these moments if I had understood them. That instant of the Prayer of Union lasted no longer than it takes to say an Ave Maria, but its effect lingered. I recognized that I had risen above the world, and I remember having regrets for others who were still distracted by earthly things.

—LIFE

march 4

·

I am in Toledo now. This is the year of the vigil of our Lady's feast in March. My health has not been better in forty years and I am able to keep the observance with all the others, which involves abstaining from meat except when it becomes absolutely necessary.

Last year I had chronic fever that returned every fourth day, but it left me feeling better. I was busy establishing the foundation in Valladolid. When the Lord thinks health is important, he gives it. When it is not, one may be ill. May God be blessed for everything.

Managing business is now a familiar routine for me. I have become skilled at bargaining and decision-making. I know what is happening in these houses of God. I think your business dealings are those of our Lord, and I am glad I know what to do. I get tired, but when I consider the good these houses bring to their communities I want to do all I can.

—LETTER TO LORENZO DE CEPEDA, 1570

march 5

People seem to trust me. Some will lend me one or two thousand ducats. Now that I have come to despise money and business deals, the Lord makes me actively involved with almost nothing else. This is not a small cross to bear. May my service in these things please His Majesty.

I find miserable people everywhere I go. Animals have better lives than we do. We are ignorant of the great dignity of our soul. We do not value it as highly as cheap earthly things. Lord, inspire us with your light.

—LETTER TO JUANA DE AHUMADA, 1569

march 6

No sister may make any remark about the quantity and quality of her food. It is our responsibility to be sure the food we provide from the Lord's provisions is properly prepared. The nuns will manage to survive because they have nothing else to eat. If an individual should have special needs regarding food and clothing, she can report it to a superior. If they require anything extraordinary, even though it may not be great, they should first turn to the Lord. Our human nature frequently desires more than it needs.

—Constitutions

march 7

I am the product of a loving home. My brothers and sisters never attempted to interfere with my desire to serve God. The brother nearest my own age was my best friend. We often read the lives of the saints together. Reading about female saints who became martyrs for God's sake, I determined that death was a small price to pay for the extreme pleasure of heaven.

I sincerely wanted to be martyred. I don't think this was the result of holy devotion. I simply wanted to experience first-hand what I read about in books. My brother would discuss with me how we could achieve martyrdom. It seems to me that the Lord had given us, as children, the courage to do this. The only thing that prevented us was our respect for our parents.

—Life

march 8
·

Pay no attention to your desire to stop after only a little time in prayer. Instead, praise the Lord that you want to pray at all. Remind yourself that you enjoy being with God. Forceful self-control is not good when you are down in the dumps. The best thing for you to do is to relax.

Take a walk outdoors under the sky. This will not harm your prayer.

Accept your weakness, making no attempt to constrain your human nature. We may seek God anywhere all the time. The soul needs to be led gently.

—LETTER TO TEUTONIO DE BRAGANZA, 1574

march 9
·

I frequently felt as though I had a store of great treasure. I wanted to share it with everyone, but my hands were tied. The favors the Lord was granting me seemed to isolate my soul. It seemed to me that I was not using these gifts for any good purpose.

Then Fray Alonso Maldonado, a Franciscan friar and great servant of God, visited me. His interest in helping others was as strong as my own. The difference was that he was able to make effective progress fulfilling his desire.

He had recently returned from the West Indies where millions of souls were being lost without Christian instruction. When he told me about this I was overcome with grief. I went to a hermitage and tearfully asked the Lord to make it possible for me to win some souls for Christ. If I was not able to do anything else, at least my prayer might be beneficial. I envied those who risked their lives as missionaries. When I read the lives of the saints and how they converted souls, I feel deep and tender devotion.

—Foundations

march 10

•

The nuns here at the Incarnation convent have improved, living quietly together. Our Lord be praised for the way he has changed them. The individuals most reluctant to accept me are now cooperative. I have ruled that we have no visitors during Lent—not even parents—which is a radical idea for this house. Even so, they accept it without complaint. Great servants of God live here and most of the nuns are improving.

Our Lady, whose statue I placed in the chair of the prioress, is working these wonders.

—LETTER TO MARÍA DE MENDOZA, 1572

march 11

•

As I prayed, I tried to keep Jesus Christ present within me. I would imagine a scene from the Gospels. But my weak imagination never succeeded in allowing me to meditate thoroughly on our Lord's life. My highest pleasure came from reading good books. Since God did not equip me with a talent for figuring things out on my own, books were an enormous help.

Others attempt to use my kind of conceptual emptiness as a way into a state of contemplation. Perhaps it works for them, but I find it to be a laborious and painful path. When one's will is not occupied and one's heart is not engaged, one's soul drifts without support or motivation.

If you consider the nature of the physical world and ponder how much you owe Jesus, who suffered for you, you will gain the tools you need to protect yourself against your own dangerous thoughts. If you are not able to conceptualize while praying, you are at risk. Compensate for this by spending more time reading. Even a little reading will replace the mental prayer that seems impossible for you. Good books assist recollection.

—LIFE

march 12

·

When I prayed one night, greatly afflicted, our Lord visited me in his usual way. He loved me tenderly, wanting to comfort me. He said, "Be patient, little daughter. You will see great things."

I never forgot these words. They burned into my heart. I had no idea how God would fulfill this promise, but it consoled me. I was sure these words would turn out to be true. I remained mystified for six months.

Since our leaders live in Rome and never come to Spain, it seemed beyond hope that one would ever visit us.

But since nothing the Lord desires is impossible, something extraordinary happened. Fray Juan Bautista Rubeo de Ravena, our father general, came to see me.

I feared he would disapprove of the changes I'd made and that he would order me back to the Incarnation where they observe the easy rule. If I returned to the Incarnation I would not be able to practice the austerity of the primitive rule. More than a hundred and fifty nuns live there. It is quieter and less stressful where only a few reside.

Our Lord amazes me. The father general is a discreet and well-educated servant of God. He thought that my work was worthwhile and did not criticize.

—FOUNDATIONS

march 13

·

When Father General de Ravena arrived in Avila, I invited him to St. Joseph's. I gave him a completely open and honest account of my life and spiritual condition, wretched as it was. He consoled me and assured me he had no intention of ordering me to leave St. Joseph's.

He approved of our manner of life and our dedication to keeping the primitive rule. No other monastery was doing this. He was so pleased he gave me letters that would allow me to establish more monasteries. Without my asking, he provided me with documentation that would prevent any provincial leader from restraining me.

I was a little shy, feeling that I should be a retiring little woman who didn't think she could do anything. But when desires such as mine enter a soul, there is no way to ignore them. Faith and a desire to please God make what seems to be unreasonable entirely possible. If our Most Reverend General wanted me to found more monasteries, I would see to it.

Then I remembered what our Lord said to me. "Be patient, little daughter. You will see great things."
—FOUNDATIONS

march 14

Now I realize God blessed me by keeping me away from a spiritual director at the beginning. If I had found one, my eighteen years of spiritual aridity and my inability to meditate would have become unendurable. All those years I always sat down to pray with a book nearby. Like an unarmed soldier in combat, I was afraid to pray without access to a book. Books were my companions, my consolation, and my shield against wildly wandering thoughts.

Without a book I would be lost. As soon as I found something worth reading, my soul began to come alive.

Words on the page lured my soul the way bait attracts fish. Sometimes it was sufficient merely to have a book within reach—I didn't even need to open it. I might read a few lines and then sometimes I would read a lot, depending on God's mercy.

—LIFE

march 15

•

The grace of the Holy Spirit be with you, padre and *señor mío.*

I have learned the house of Juan de Avila de la Vega is for sale. I think it will perfectly suit our needs. Both the price and the location are excellent. It is also located near you.

The house is old enough to require extensive repair. That is not a barrier since it has plenty of space and a good well. Please begin to negotiate the purchase of this property for us, but don't appear to be too eager. That will make them raise the price.

—LETTER TO BALTASAR ALVAREZ, 1575

march 16

•

I praise and bless you, my Lord. You took the filthy mud I am and turned it into clear water that you could serve at your table.

How remarkable you are when you reach out your hand to lift up a soul who has fallen even after you cleansed it. Any such soul knows the dimension of your greatness and mercy as well as its own misery.

All of your gifts are undeserved.

—LIFE

march 17

•

I was a poor shoeless nun with no help other than the Lord's. I had a stack of formal permission letters and a good desire to build monasteries, but no openings anywhere. Even though there seemed to be no possibility of getting anything started, my courage and hope never weakened. If the Lord gave one thing, he would also give the other. Believing that everything was possible, I got busy.

O the greatness of God! You give courage to a mere ant. When we fail to accomplish great assignments it is not because of you. Our own timidity prevents you from working through us. You enjoy giving and serving even at great cost to yourself, if someone is willing to receive your favors. Please let me do something for you and not have to account for all that I have received. Amen.

—FOUNDATIONS

march 18

One nun should not criticize another for her mistakes. If her faults are serious, counsel her gently. Attempt to correct her lovingly three times. If she does not respond, tell the mother prioress, but no one else.

Because some sisters serve as monitors who watch for misbehavior, there is no need for the remainder to worry about this. Let them be mindful of their own faults.

They should also ignore mistakes committed by anyone leading worship, unless it is a serious infraction. Instead, they should avoid excusing themselves for similar blunders. This will be a beneficial practice.

—CONSTITUTIONS

march 19

•

When someone has the spirit of prayer, she has a strong desire to be in one of these houses. There are no more than thirteen nuns in any of them.

Our constitution does not allow us to ask for alms. We eat what we receive.

I think you will be glad when you visit these houses. Regarding those things that are given, no one insists on an accounting.

I pray for my brother, Agustín de Ahumada, because I have no idea how he is getting along with our Lord. I pray a lot for him.

—LETTER TO LORENZO DE CEPEDA, 1570

march 20
·

When others learned of my intention to build a monastery, I received a lot of criticism. A few said I was crazy. Many hoped I wouldn't do anything. Even the bishop admitted later that he thought I was foolish. He did not say that to anyone, and he made no effort to stop me.

My friends also denigrated my project. I paid no attention to them because I believed what they thought was impossible would turn out to be easy. I had no thought that I might fail. The Lord was taking care of all the details.

—FOUNDATIONS

march 21
·

I am sorry about the falls you have had. Perhaps they should tie you in the saddle! What kind of donkey do you have? Why do you need to travel ten leagues a day on a pack saddle? That's murderous.

It's turning colder now. Have you remembered to put on more clothes? I pray to God that you have suffered no harm. Because you enjoy helping others, think of the loss they would experience if you became incapacitated.

For the love of God, take care of yourself!

—LETTER TO JERÓNIMO GRACIÁN, CA. 1575

march 22

·

My Redeemer, when I think about the divisions in your church I am greatly distressed. What's happening to us? We who are most indebted to you bring you the most trouble. You have been kind to us, you choose us to be your friends, you move among us, nurturing us with the sacraments. Still, we cause you grief.

Today, my Lord, there is no sacrifice in withdrawing from the world. If worldly people do not respect you, how can we expect them to care about us? Why should we think they would treat us better than they treat you?

—WAY

march 23

During my novice year at the convent I worried a lot about small things. I did not handle it well when anyone blamed me for trouble that was not my fault. It hurt me deeply. Only my joy at being a nun enabled me to endure unjust accusations. If someone were to observe my tears as I prayed, they would conclude that I was not adjusting to life in the convent. This was not true. I embraced the religious life with joy. What I really wanted was their respect. This kind of misunderstanding brought me pain.

—LIFE

march 24

We are wrong when we build great houses with poor people's money. God forbid. Our houses should be small and simple in every detail. We are to be like our King, who was born in a stable at Bethlehem and died on a cross. Such houses provide slight comfort.

Sometimes well-intentioned people build large houses, but any corner is enough for thirteen poor women. We may have a few small hermitages where sisters may pray, but God spare us from building a grand ornate convent with many buildings.

Such places will collapse on the Day of Judgment. It would not be good if the house of thirteen poor women made a great crash when it fell. Those who are truly poor are quiet, living an inconspicuous life.

—WAY

march 25

•

It disturbed me for anyone to think I was a good person. I composed a special prayer for such moments, asking God to reveal my sins. I didn't want someone believing I was receiving divine favors because I had earned them. I wanted everyone to know I was an undeserving recipient of God's amazing grace.

My spiritual director did not like this special prayer, but I continued to use it until very recently. When someone began to express admiration, I would look for ways to display my sins. I found relief in this, but my confessor disapproved it. He has made me a little more reticent about this.

Now I understand my reaction did not result from humility, but from a subtle kind of temptation. My immature spirituality caused this. Those who are completely surrendered to God simply don't care what others may think or say about them.

—LIFE

march 26

A young priest lived in my sister's village. His family was respected and he had extraordinary intelligence. He was well educated, but not to an excess. I began to visit him for confession. I have always been attracted to learned men. It has been difficult for me to find one who is as well educated as I would like. A genuinely educated man has never misled me.

I believe ignorant men are less dangerous than those with a little learning. If they are virtuous and holy, they are better with no knowledge from books or classrooms. If they lack confidence they will confer with others who are better educated.

Poorly educated men do not consciously try to deceive me, but they don't know what they are doing. In my early years I assumed they did and that I was required to believe them. They spoke in vague terms and did not set limits. If they'd been strict, I would no doubt have gone looking for someone who would tell me what I wanted to hear.

My spiritual guides would insist that my minor sins were not serious and that my major sins were minor. I am writing about this in order to warn others to avoid incompetent spiritual directors.

—LIFE

march 27

•

By repeating what my inept teachers had told me, I misguided many others. I wandered in this wilderness for more than seventeen years, when Vicente Barrón, a Dominican friar, showed me a better path. This well-educated man convinced me I was living with religious illusions. Some Jesuit priests corroborated what he said.

The priest in my sister's village whom I turned to for confession indicated that he was attracted to me. His affection for me was wrong only because it was so strong. He understood I would never behave in a manner offensive to God, who had become my center of interest.

The priest began to speak to me confidentially of his own problems. He admitted he had been close to a woman in the village for nearly seven years. Everyone knew about his affair, but he continued to celebrate Mass. His reputation was ruined, but no one turned him in.

I was genuinely sorry for him and considered him a good friend. My idea was that it was virtuous to support anyone who was my friend. Such loyalty is damnable when it distracts us from loyalty to God. I am shocked by the way we will act against God in order to prevent straining a human friendship.

—LIFE

march 28

•

As I talked with others about my priest, I discovered that he had become seriously entangled with the woman. She had pretended to cast a spell on him by giving him a small copper charm and urging him to wear it around his neck as a token of their love. He wore it all the time.

I am warning other men to be cautious. There are women who will compromise themselves before God to gain selfish control over you. Forcing affection through manipulation is not love.

After learning about the "spell," I personally supported this priest. I had good intentions, but I did not know the best ways to do this. Most of my conversation with him was about God, but his love for me seemed to help him the most. Finally, he handed me the copper amulet and I threw it in the river.

The priest seemed as though waking from a dream. He began to tell me about all of his experiences with the other woman, admitting his disappointment with himself. He ended his relationship with her, thanking God for bringing him to his senses.

—LIFE

march 29

·

On the anniversary of my meeting that priest who had been trapped, he died. I did not think there was anything amiss with his fondness for me, even though it could have been purer. There had been moments when only his commitment to God prevented serious offense. He knew I scrupulously avoided offending God, which only increased his love for me.

All men are attracted to virtuous women. Women who have no interests beyond this world will discover increasing interest from men if they keep their integrity. The priest I mentioned died a holy death, far beyond the mistakes he had made. The Lord used his sin to redeem him.

He had been most diligent in the service of God; and as for that great affection he had for me, I never observed anything wrong in it, though it might have been of greater purity. There were also occasions when he might have gotten into greater trouble, if he hadn't kept himself in the near presence of God. As I said before, I wouldn't have done anything I knew was a mortal sin. And I think that observing this resolution in me helped him to have that affection.

Women must have more power over men because they are good, as I shall show later. I am convinced that the priest is in the way of salvation. He died most piously and completely withdrawn from any occasion of sin. It seems that it was the will of our Lord that he should be saved by these means.

—LIFE

march 30

·

Today people are not tired of living even if they make it to a hundred years old. They continue to desire a longer life. But our lives are not as difficult as the one Jesus lived. We don't have to carry the burdens of trials and poverty he had to bear. His life was always like dying. He knew a cross was waiting for him. He saw how far away people were from his Father. His great love made this deeply painful for him. He prayed, "And do not bring us to the time of trial, but rescue us from the evil one" (Matt. 6:13). He wanted his Father to spare him so many evils and trials here and give him eternal rest in his kingdom.

There is no way we can be free from temptation and imperfection. But I pray, Lord, that you deliver me from evil forever. I owe more than I can pay and I am deeper in debt every day. I am never sure if the things I want are acceptable in your sight. Deliver me, Lord, from evil.

—WAY

In the cross there is life
And also consolation.
It stands alone on the road
Showing the way to heaven.

On that cross is the Lord
Of heaven and earth,
And it holds much peace.
While wars destroy,
It drives out all evil
Here on earth.
It stands alone on the road
Showing the way to heaven.

It is an olive tree,
This holy cross,
That anoints us with its oil
And gives us light.
My soul, take up the cross
With great consolation.
It stands alone on the road
Showing the way to heaven.

Since he accepted the cross
Our Savior
Has given it glory
And honor.
And suffering pain,
We find life and comfort.
It stands alone on the road
Showing the way to heaven.
Like an unarmed soldier in combat.

—From "El Camino de la Cruz"

april

1

You ask me to instruct you about prayer. Before I say anything specific about the interior life, I want to remind you of how to find the road to prayer.

There are some important prerequisites for seeking the way to travel. Without them it will be impossible to become a contemplative person. I will narrow them down for you to three things:

- Show love to other people.
- Be detached from the things of this world.
- And demonstrate genuine humility.

The last is the most important of all and includes the other two.

—WAY

april 2
.

I frequently remember the occasion when our Lord commanded the waves and wind to be still. If he can do that, then I ask myself, "Who is this person who controls all my faculties? Who is it that quickly helps me while I am in such profound darkness? Who softens a stony heart? Who gives gentle tears to one living in dryness? Who imparts my desires? Who provides this courage? What do I fear?"

I realize that I desire nothing other than to please him. I seek no happiness, no rest, and no other good than to do his will. I have experienced the power of the Lord. I know the devils are impotent when he is present. They cannot harm a servant of this Lord and King, and I'm brave enough to battle against all of hell.

—Life

april 3
.

M y prayer became very bold today. "I have accepted the fact that you want to keep me in this miserable world, but everything here hinders my spiritual life. I have to eat, sleep, conduct business, and converse with many people. I suffer this torment because I love you, my Lord.

"Now I am grabbing a few spare moments to be with you. Why do you hide from me, my Beloved? Abandoning me seems incompatible with my understanding of your love. Lord, I think you would not like me to hide from you this way. I am sure you are with me all the time. Don't let me experience this loneliness any longer. You are hurting one who deeply loves you."

Sometimes my love for God makes me say crazy things. I praise God for putting up with me.

—LIFE

april 4

.

Audit your financial records carefully. Expenses must not exceed income even if the community has to get along without something. If we spend according to our resources we will have enough and get along splendidly, praise God. Borrowing money will gradually ruin us. I would rather see a monastery dissolved than to see it in debt. Carelessness in financial practices can bring great harm to spiritual matters.

What I have said is most important. Stay out of debt. If nuns have faith and serve God, they will never lack anything—unless they spend too much.

—Visitation

april 5

Consider an orchard in spring. See how the trees are taking on new life. Soon they will blossom and bear fruit. It is good to think of your soul as such a place. Imagine the Lord walking in it. Ask him to increase the fragrance of the little virtuous buds that are beginning to appear. Beg him to keep them alive until they can bloom to his glory. Invite him to prune away whatever he thinks needs to go. The trees will be better if he does.

A time will come to the soul when it is like an overgrown orchard. Everything seems dry and lifeless. It is hard to believe it was ever thriving and flourishing. The soul suffers many trials. The poor orchardist thinks it is out of control. It appears hopelessly lost.

This is the proper time for cultivation. Remove the weeds. Root out sickly plants, making room for healthy trees. If we do this we can gain much humility, and then the blossoms will come again.

—WAY

april 6

Please speak cautiously even if you have some complaints about the papal nuncio. I am well aware of your frankness and I know you can be careless about this. I pray that he will not hear anything you have said. The devils are at war with us. Look only to God for support. We do this by obeying and suffering until God takes charge.

When Passion Sunday comes, you and the other shoeless friars should go to your monastery in Pastrana or Alcalá. This is not the time to do business. If there is anything that can't wait, let Juan Calvo de Padilla take care of it. It is not good for us to be outside during these holy days.

Avoid speaking to the archbishop. Insist on nothing. He has accepted responsibility; leave it to him. The best way for you to take care of this business is to remain silent and speak with God.

I have given a lot of thought to this letter, and I am sure I am asking you to do the right thing. No harm will come to us if you do as I instruct, and much will come if you ignore me. I have seen you control your temper. Prudence demands that you control it now.

—LETTER TO AMBROSIO MARIANO, 1577

april 7

Mutual love makes it possible to bear irritations. Only exceptionally bad behavior will annoy you. But perfect love among people requires a delicate balance.

It is possible to have too little or too much love. You may think it is not possible to have too much love, but it can lead to evil when we think we are acting virtuously. Perhaps we may not love each other equally or may feel resentful when a friend is hurt. Also, intimate friendships do not often concentrate on love of God. The devil uses such friendships to create factions among us.

Let's all be friends with each other, love each other, and help each other. Avoid close individual friendships, which can become toxic. This may seem harsh, but my advice will result in great peace. Don't become overly attached to anyone other than Christ.

—WAY

april 8

.

I am thankful that God blessed me with much patience. This gift came directly from God. I read about Job in *The Morals of Saint Gregory*, which greatly increased my patience. I even slept with this book. The Lord used this writing to get me ready for more suffering to come. Developing contemplative prayer also helped me. My conversations were with God, and I carried Job's words in my mind: "Shall we receive the good at the hand of God, and not receive the bad?" (Job 2:10). I gained strength by repeating this verse often.

I was in a coma for nearly four days. They administered extreme unction, expecting me to die. They must have concluded that I *was* dead, because when I woke up I discovered wax on my eyelids. They had dug a grave for me behind the Incarnation, and a distant monastery had performed last rites for me. But God was pleased to restore my consciousness. My first thought was to go to confession—and Communion brought tears to my eyes.

—LIFE

april 9

I shudder when I remember how God brought me back to life. I say to my soul, "It would be good for you to recall the danger from which the Lord delivered you. Then, if love is not sufficient to keep you from offending him, awe may prompt you. You have escaped a thousand perils greater than the physical condition you were in back then."

"A thousand" is not an exaggeration. The one who ordered me to write the story of my life advised me to be circumspect when I write of my sins. I have presented myself too innocently up to this point. I ask this man, for the love of God, to leave my faults as they are. They are an indication of God's magnificence and willingness to suffer for us.

Let us bless God forever!

—LIFE

april 10

Others often accused me of imagining spiritual things or even succumbing to the devil. Some of my critics were deeply devout. In comparison with them, I was a lost soul. Since God was taking them down another path, they could not recognize my experiences and found them frightening. I told only a few people what was happening to me, but the word soon got around.

I attempted to affirm the validity of my experience with this analogy: "If you tried to make me think I was mistaken about the identity of someone I had finished talking with, I might be persuaded. But if that individual had given me some valuable jewelry as a token of his love, I could not possibly believe what you suggest. I was poor before we conversed and now I am rich."

My visions left jewels in my soul that totally changed me. Even my critics could see the transformation because God's blessing touched every area of my life. This was not something I could pretend, and they knew it was genuine.

—LIFE

april 11

A convent infirmary is not a lonely place. While I was there, when I spoke, I talked about God. I refused to say anything about another person that I would not want said of me. Anyone who spent some time with me determined they would practice this also. In other areas, I set a poor example and I will be accountable to God.

My desire for solitude remains strong. I continue to enjoy reading good books. I take Communion and make confession frequently. Sometimes I avoid prayer because I do not want to face my disloyalty to God.

When I was an invalid I was still quite young. Realizing no doctor would be able to help me, I sought heavenly healing. I had forced myself to endure sickness with joy, but I wanted to get better in order to be of more service to God.

—LIFE

april 12

•

I trust God that if you are considerate toward this padre he will understand you have restored him to your good graces. Everything will then work out well. You will receive a letter from him. He really wants to please you and thinks of himself as your obedient son.

I ask that when you answer him, you will be gentle and not mention past events. Even though he may bear some responsibility, receive him as the son and subject he really is.

His letter may not convey his thoughts because he is not able to express himself clearly. He assures me he never intended to offend you in any way.

Typically, sons make mistakes and fathers forgive them, overlooking their faults. For the love of our Lord, I ask you to grant me this favor. No harm can come from being receptive to those who cast themselves at your feet. God always forgives. It will hurt nothing if you tell him you are pleased the reform can be done by one of your sons and subjects, and because of this, you are pleased to forgive him.

—LETTER TO JUAN BAUTISTA RUBEO, 1576

april 13

When we want someone's affection, it is usually because we seek profit or pleasure for ourselves. These are the things those who are perfect have crushed beneath their feet. They have no interest in the delights of this world and concern themselves with God alone. The return of affection is like straw blown about by the wind.

This does not result in a lessening of love for anyone other than God. In fact, they will love others much more than formerly and with a more genuine love. They will love with greater fervor and receive more than ever before. This defines true love. Such souls would rather give than receive even in their divine relationship.

"Love" is, above all, holy affection. Those with lower interests in loving have stolen the name.

—WAY

W e needed to act quickly. I expected some opposition because of my experience with the first foundation. I wanted to take possession of the house we had selected before anyone else discovered what we were doing.

It was midnight when we arrived in Medina del Campo. We dismounted quietly at St. Anne's and walked to the house.

God had much mercy on us because we had to pass through an area where bulls had been corralled for a run the next day. We were so eager to get to our new house we did not consider the bulls. The Lord, who faithfully looks out for those who are trying to serve him, prevented the bulls from charging and striking us.

When we entered the courtyard, I noticed the walls were dilapidated. When the sun came up they looked worse than I thought. We had to clear debris from the entrance. We had about three blankets, which were not enough to cover the openings. There was no place suitable for an altar. The Lord was pleased to motivate the former owner to send her butler with an armful of tapestries and a blue damask bedspread. This good lady instructed him to give us whatever we needed.

All of us praised the Lord when we saw such nice things. There was no way we could buy nails in the wee hours of the morning, but I found a stash of them in the wall. We hung the tapestries and cleaned the floor. By dawn the next day, the altar was in place and we had a little bell in a corridor. By saying Mass, we could officially take possession. Because I did not understand this, we partook of the reserved Blessed Sacrament. I was greatly pleased to have one more church where this could be done.

—FOUNDATIONS

april 15

Our life is fraught with hazards, Lord. You have held my hand for many years. I have tried to place your will ahead of my own in things both great and small. Over the years you have tested my resolution and I am sure that I've often disappointed you.

I am your servant. You have helped me accomplish many things. I desire nothing of this world's goods. The only things that make me happy come from you. All else feels like a heavy cross.

Perhaps I am mistaken. Maybe I'm not sincere when I report what I want. My Beloved, you know I'm not lying. Please don't give up on me. I totally depend upon your grace to make up the difference for my lack of ability and virtue.

Please do not abandon me. In the past I thought it would be impossible for me ever to turn away from you, but I did. This frightens me because when you withdraw from me even a little bit, I fall flat on my face. When I neglect you, you offer your hand and help me back up. Sometimes I refused to accept it, but you always called again.

—LIFE

april 16

Unless you experience it, you will never believe the joy we feel when we are isolated from the secular world. No matter how much we love anyone on the outside, it is not enough to make us wish we were not alone.

It's like pulling a net full of fish from a river. There is no life for them squirming in that net, but only if they are released into the water again. We who become accustomed to living in the flowing streams of our Spouse simply can't live again if we are caught in a net of worldly things.

A nun who wants to go out and converse a lot with secular people should be concerned that they may not have discovered the "living water" our Lord mentioned to the Samaritan woman at the well.

—FOUNDATIONS

april 17

I surrendered to many subtle and destructive temptations. My soul drifted far from God on a river of vanity. I did not want to be near God. Prayer is intimacy with the divine, and I felt unworthy. The more mistakes I made, the lower my self-image became. Holy things were of little comfort in my sinful state.

Beloved God, my joy diminished because I was failing you. Evil masqueraded as humility and led me into the most insidious deception of them all—a fear of prayer. It seemed to me that I was the wickedest person on earth and that I should abandon silent contemplation and return to a familiar routine of prayer. Instead of private conversation with God, I would recite the spoken prayers I had been taught. I did not want to be seen praying silently because I did not want anyone to think I was a holy person when I knew I was not. It bothered me more to think that others would be fooled by my exterior appearance of goodness than that they would clearly see the truth about my interior life.

—LIFE

april 18

If a nun asks for a transfer to another monastery, answer in a way that will not give anyone the slightest idea that this could be possible. Experience teaches us how much trouble can result from even a small crack in the door. Nuns will be tempted when they think it is possible to move from one monastery to another. Regardless of the strength of their reason to request relocation, it must seem beyond hope. If you grant a transfer, the nun must have no idea of the reason or think it was because she requested it.

Unless we practice subterfuge the nun will never settle down anywhere. This is harmful to the other nuns. Let the nuns understand that desire for relocation will work against them.

It may be best to present this idea to the entire community rather than to one troubled individual. Please be sure to explain our reasoning carefully to everyone.

—Visitation

april 19
.

Make every effort to remember what you were like when you were weak. Keep in mind that if you are not weak now, this is not your achievement. If you don't, you will gradually be tempted to look down on others, and you will view this personal failing as a sign of perfection. Stay alert regarding this. The devil never sleeps. The nearer we approach perfection, the more careful we need to be. Harm can come before we realize what is happening. Always watch and pray. Prayer is the best way to discover the increasingly clever secret schemes of our adversary.

—WAY

april 20

It may have been a mistake for me to live at first in an uncloistered convent. Those who have not taken a vow of enclosure have more opportunity for going astray. Most women are trustworthy and do not take advantage of their freedom, but I am bad. Ultimately the only reason this lack of restriction didn't lead me to hell was that the Lord looked out for me.

The less regulated the spiritual community, the greater the risks. Personal liberty can be a trap.

We practice strict spiritual discipline where I am now, but there are houses that enforce few rules, which breaks my heart. If life in a convent resembles that of the rest of the world, the nuns easily neglect their religious obligations. The Lord stays busy trying to remind them why they are there.

—LIFE

april 21

Our critics objected to everything imaginable having to do with our project. I could see they had a point. It seemed that there was no need for me to continue this work. Earlier I had believed I could accomplish anything for the Lord, but now I didn't think I could finish what I had started. This limited God's flow of power. All I could see was my own weakness and inferiority.

If I had been by myself the agony may have been manageable. But I had all these others with me, and they had come with me against serious opposition. It troubled me to think of them returning sheepishly to their former houses. How could I help? If my first assignment failed, my plans for the future must also crumble. Perhaps what I had understood when I prayed was an illusion. This thought was the most painful of all. Had the devil deceived me?

O my God, it is awesome to see a soul you have abandoned to suffering. When I remember this time, and others like it during the making of these foundations, I don't think great physical pain can compare with spiritual pain.

—FOUNDATIONS

april 22

Parents should not think their daughters would immediately walk in the way of God if they send them to a convent. They are probably more likely to get into trouble there than out in the world.

If young women are sincerely devout, God may lead them away from danger and toward what is good. If they are not, they would be better staying at home. They would not be able to hide their behavior very well at home, but in a monastic environment they can live concealed for a long time.

—LIFE

april 23

Some girls enter a spiritual community with an idea that they might escape the hazards of life in the ordinary world. They expect to serve God with no distractions. Before they know what happened, they are entangled in ten worlds and see no way out. Youth, sensuality, and fallen nature mislead these young women. They are like atheists who try to avoid the sacred and then want to convince others they are following the only sensible path, even as a voice deep within them whispers a contrary truth.

Great harm comes when we do not live what we profess. This applies to both men and women. When we enter a religious life we have a choice of following a course of virtue and devotion or not. I've seen it done both ways, with most people following an irreligious path because it is the widest and easiest. A true spiritual life is rare.

—Life

april 24

•

While I was in Medina, my mind continued to think about monasteries for friars, which I did not have. I discussed this privately with the prior at Medina and asked for his guidance. He was delighted and offered to be my first friar. I told him he must be joking. I knew he was a good man, recollected, educated, and fond of his cell, but he did not seem to me to be the one to help me start a new work. I did not think his health was strong enough to endure austerity. He assured me he was serious and that the Lord was calling him to a stricter life. He had already determined he would transfer to the Carthusians, and they had signaled their acceptance of him. Still, I was not satisfied. I told him to begin practicing what he thought he wanted to do. He did this for a year and suffered many trials. He dealt with the persecution and false accusations in an admirable manner, making me believe His Majesty was grooming him for the new foundation.

Meanwhile, two young priests came for a visit. One told me wonderful things about the life of the other, who was a student at Salamanca. This young father was named John of the Cross. I praised the Lord when I heard this report. When I spoke with him, he pleased me very much. He told me he wanted to become a Carthusian. Relating my own plans, I urged him to hold off until the Lord allowed me to found a monastery. I told him that if he wanted to strengthen his spiritual life, it would be good for him to remain in his present order. That way he could render much greater service to the Lord.

—FOUNDATIONS

april 25

The world does not have a high regard for prayer and perfection. Others already hesitate to follow the path of prayer. Why should I make them more cautious by mentioning hazards along the way? Perhaps I need to explain myself carefully. The truth is there is risk in everything we do. We must proceed with caution, asking the Lord to instruct us and remain our companion. We reduce the danger when we keep our minds focused on God.

We notice, my Lord, that you often help us escape the consequences of our own mistakes. We cannot believe you will fail to assist us when we want nothing more than to please you and delight in you. Good never results in evil. May what I have said help us walk more confidently along the path of prayer so that we may more quickly discover and please our Spouse. Let none of my cautions cause anyone to abandon this path. Give us the courage to pray.

—Foundations

A ny concern you may have regarding the temptation of egotism is pointless. Care about spiritual pride may be the design of the devil, who wants us to be anxious. He distorts this natural reticence in order to keep our spiritual desire unseen, while he encourages the unrighteous to flaunt their sins. Offenses against God are so common today that people talk openly about them. They even seem to enjoy them.

We are so negligent of spiritual matters that those of us who know and serve God need to support each other. Unless we have this kind of companionship we will not make much progress. This is why holy men and women withdrew to the desert long ago. Christian love increases when we share it. A thousand blessings blossom like flowers in a garden. I had many friends who helped me fall, but there was no one to help me get to my feet. Only God gave me a hand.

—LIFE

april 27

Near the beginning of a personal relationship, the Lord found a way to convince me that this association was not good for me. He penetrated my thick blindness in order to teach and guide me. I saw Christ himself standing in front of me. He emphatically told me what was wrong with such relationships. I saw him more clearly with my spiritual eyes than I could ever see him with physical eyes. This vision was so impressive that twenty-six years later I clearly recall it. I was stunned and disturbed. I never wanted to see that other person again.

There is no way I can convince myself that it would be impossible to see anything other than what is perceived through open eyes. I wondered if that vision of Christ could have been a figment of my imagination or something demonic, but I remain convinced that the vision came from God and was not imaginary.

The sternness of Christ as I saw him displeased me. I tried to forget it, and I did not talk with others about the experience. I admitted to myself that I could not see anything wrong with my relationship with that other person.

I began to have close conversations with him about this and enjoyed visits from others. I kept this up for years and it never seemed to be a mistake. None of the others distracted me as much as the individual I mentioned above. I was inordinately fond of him.

—LIFE

april 28

Be compassionate. When you spot faults in others, show courteous sympathy. It is both a test and a proof of your love that you can observe such faults without experiencing shock. Others will have an opportunity to bear with your faults, many of which you may not recognize yourself. Pray for anyone who has a vice and try to practice its opposite virtue. Your actions will teach others far better than your words and suffering.

Look for good in others. Don't forget this. One person's love can help others. If you become angry and speak hastily, correct yourself immediately and pray resolutely. This also applies to grudges you may have or your desire to be the greatest. Understand that you have driven your Spouse from his home. Cry out to Christ and correct yourself.

—WAY

april 29

The mail carrier leaves tomorrow, but I had decided not to write you because I didn't have any good news to send. Just before we shut the door tonight, I received word that the man who lives in the house agrees that we may come in two days, May 1, the feast of saints Philip and James. I believe the Lord is softening our trials.

Pass this message along to Mother Prioress in Medina. I know she is worried by what I wrote in an earlier letter, even though I did not exaggerate the difficulties we are experiencing here. When you hear a report, you will know things will work out well here only by the mercy of God. Injustice is commonplace in this region. I have never before seen so much dishonesty and treachery. These people have earned their poor reputation.

If my brother Lorenzo were not here, we would have accomplished nothing. He has paid a dear price for helping us. No one else supported us. Lorenzo is in hiding now because of his relationship with us. He barely escaped a jail sentence. Prisons here are hellish. There is no justice. They want us to pay an illegal excise tax on our purchase of a house, and they threatened my brother with imprisonment because he had given surety. The only solution for this will have to come from Madrid. He is pleased to suffer something for God.

Lorenzo lingers in the Carmelite monastery with our Padre Gracián, on whom problems are falling like hail. I try to hide our own trials from him.

—LETTER TO MARÍA BAUTISTA, 1576

april 30

•

Beginners often want to help others before they have learned how to take care of themselves. I fell into that trap. I loved my father and wanted him to have the blessings I was enjoying when I prayed. This seemed like the best gift to share with him.

I did my best to get him to pray. I gave him books about prayer. He took me up on it and in a few years was making great progress. I praised God. Father frequently visited me and discussed divine things with me.

At the same time, I was failing. My own prayer life had grown dull. It hurt me to see that my father thought I was practicing what I preached. I had even convinced myself that abstaining from prayer showed more humility—which resulted in a year without prayer. At last, I told my father the truth, using my health as the excuse.

—LIFE

may

1
•

God has blessed us by bringing us together here. The twelve of us are one. It is impossible for me to hide my wickedness in such an intimate setting. God has gathered us for his service. Nuns in other convents have more freedom, but not more spiritual liberty or perfect peace. Anyone who does not want this should not try to live here.

Visits by relatives that feel like crosses to bear are permissible. It will help the visitors and do no harm for any of us. On the other hand, if you relish their visits, and if their reports of trouble distress you while their stories about life in the world please you, you are harming yourself and doing them no good.

—WAY

may 2

Our Lord always gives us an opportunity to pray. We can pray while we are engaged in daily activities. We also use sickness and distress as an offering to God. The only thing we are required to do is to accept what comes our way.

Prayer is love in action. We are mistaken when we believe we must be quietly alone in order to pray. Anyway, we often waste our time when we are in private. If we will work at it, we will discover great blessings in all the circumstances in which our Lord places us. If we seize every opportunity, we will not find it difficult to uncover these blessings.

—LIFE

may 3

Nothing bothers me at the moment. I can't imagine where this is leading. I have a private cell that is set apart like a happy hermitage. I am in excellent health and isolated from relatives who stay in touch through letters. You had an excellent idea when you let me remain here. I feel unusually confident.

I read the story of Moses in Exodus last night. The troublesome plagues that bothered an entire kingdom did not touch him. Nothing is able to bother us if the Lord does not allow it. The narrative about crossing the Red Sea brought me delight because I realize how we are asking for a lot less than that.

I am returning to my preparation of the *Foundations*. With God's help it will be useful to others. I am grateful that you ordered me to write it. I think the Lord is helping us, and I ask that my work may bring him glory and benefit many souls.

—LETTER TO JERÓNIMO GRACIÁN, 1576

may 4
.

If you are beginning a life of prayer, I advise you to get together with others who share your interest. This can be extremely helpful because we can help each other. Typical human friendship results in relaxation and small talk, which is good and is comforting. I would not discourage anyone who is beginning to love and serve God from socializing in order to discuss the difficulties and pleasures of following a spiritual path.

Such discussion brings no risk because if you have an authentic friendship with God, you don't need to worry about self-interests. Admit them as soon as they appear and you will conquer them. Discussing such things with similarly minded friends will help both you and others.

There is no way I can emphasize the importance of such friendships too much. When we are not yet spiritually ripe, we have plenty of friends who might help and many enemies who would like to lead us astray.

—LIFE

may 5

I struggled for twenty years, pulled in two directions. While I was involved with the world, God gave me the courage to pray. It requires courage when you know God knows all about you.

We understand that we are always in God's presence, but when you pray you are with him in a special way. You become conscious of God all the time. Most of my days include several hours for prayer, even though I divided my allegiance between God and the world.

I am telling you all of this to help you understand the mercy of God. Your commitment may be less than perfect, but if you will continue to pray God will bless you. Keep praying even when you are tempted and fail. Whatever difficulties you face, the Beloved will lead you to a safe harbor.

Good things happen when we pray because prayer restores what is broken.

—LIFE

may 6

If your vow of obedience pulls you away from a time of prayer and makes you busy with external concerns, don't be sad. The Lord is present among the pots and pans of the kitchen and will help you both interiorly and exteriorly.

I know someone who was determined never to refuse anything commanded by a superior, regardless of the labor involved. Once, at the end of the day when he was exhausted from work, he sat down for a little rest. His superior passed by and told him to do some weeding in the garden. He made no audible response even though the idea brought him pain. Obediently, he took a hoe and headed for the garden. When he came to the garden gate, our Lord appeared to him carrying the weight of his cross. This monk showed me the very spot where he saw Jesus. Compared with Christ on his way to Calvary, the monk understood his own fatigue was minor.

There is no path that will take you to perfection faster than the path of obedience. The highest perfection, after all, does not consist in pleasure, raptures, visions, or prophetic utterances. It involves conforming our desires with our understanding of God's will so that we will accept the bitter along with the sweet. This is not easy because it goes against our nature. But perfect love has the strength to do it. Then we forget about ourselves and concentrate on the one we love.

—FOUNDATIONS

·

If you have not yet started a life of prayer, I urge you, for the love of God, to seize this opportunity for a great blessing. Don't be afraid. You will only find love at this table. Perhaps you will not make rapid progress and will fail to give enough effort to realize the gifts that God lavishes upon more devoted people; you will at least catch sight of the road that leads to paradise.

If you continue to pray, I know God will have mercy on you. Contemplative prayer is an intimate exchange between friends. It is a matter of often taking time to be alone with someone who loves us, nurturing and cultivating this love. Desires and interests of both parties will resonate harmoniously. The Lord, being perfect, loves us perfectly, but our human nature remains sensual and self-centered. We are not yet able to contribute much to this beautiful friendship, experiencing pain when we understand how different we are from the object of our love.

—LIFE

may 8

God, you are infinitely good. When we are together I see myself as well as you. When I think of you, the delight of angels, you totally consume me. You graciously allow someone like me to be with you. What a friend you are, my Lord.

You are patient with us and comfort us, waiting for us to rise to our true selves. Until that happens, you accept us as we are. In one atoning instant you forget all our sins.

I have experienced this so clearly. Why won't many others turn to you? If they would ask you to be with them for about two hours a day, good things will happen. Even if they are distracted by a maelstrom of churning thoughts and distractions, as I have been, the simple act of trying to be in your presence will have positive results.

Beloved, you defend and strengthen us. You lead us to victory over ourselves and the world. You will not abandon anyone who trusts in you and desires to be your friend. You keep our bodies healthy and awaken our souls.

—LIFE

I tried for more than fourteen years to meditate without reading something. I am sure I am not alone in this. Some can't meditate even *after* reading. All they can do is recite vocal prayers, and even then their minds wander. If they attempt to focus on God, doubts and foolish thoughts about faith overwhelm them.

Other humble persons are eager to make progress. When they observe someone crying, they think they should also shed tears in order to advance. Tears are not necessarily an indicator of perfection. It is better to practice humility, sacrifice, detachment, and the other virtues.

—Way

Humility and denial of self belong together. Embrace them, love them, and keep them as your constant companions. These are the ruling virtues. They control the world and deliver us from evil. Christ loved them dearly and never lived apart from them. If you have humility and are detached from yourself, you may safely combat the armies of hell. You need not fear anyone. Instead of worrying about losing something, your only fear is that you may displease God.

Humility and denial of self are hidden from the one who has them. Someone may tell you that you possess them, but since you value them so highly you will continue trying to find them. All the time, they grow more perfect. There is no need for me to praise these virtues because the King of Glory praised them through the trials he endured.

—WAY

may 11
.

It was not easy for me to keep my attention on God when I prayed. If I had planned to pray for an hour, I listened to the ticking clock instead of quietly spending time with my Beloved. Rather than engaging in lofty thoughts, I waited for the hour to strike. It would have been easier for me to do heavy penance than to recollect myself and pray.

It used to take all the courage God ever gave me to turn aside and pray. Entering the chapel often made me sad. Once I began to meditate under these circumstances, I found more profound peace than when I voluntarily prayed. Prayer has remedied all of my troubles.

If the Lord has contended with someone like me, why should you be afraid to pray? Regardless of your history, you could not possibly have been off the track longer than I was after I received the first blessings from God. If a person like me, a habitual offender of God, has discovered everything worthwhile in prayer, why would you hesitate? Prayer will not hurt you. It always brings positive results.

—LIFE

may 12

I see that you do not understand my regard for Padre Olea. Issues regarding the acceptance of a novice at Carmel are not a matter of friendship with him, but of conscience. Padre Olea does not know the nuns there. I know they are God's servants who would never refuse to admit anyone without good reasons. The introduction of a person unsuited for religious life in a small community could be devastating. There is no way I can force them to accept her.

You amused me when you wrote that you could judge her character on sight. We women are not that easy to understand. It amazes experienced confessors to realize how little they know about us. When you want one of our houses to do you a favor by accepting someone, please send a person who is compatible with this life. When that is lacking, there is no way I can help.

I have no intention of speaking with Valdemoro, the prior of the Carmelites in Avila. I suspect that he does not intend his friendliness toward us for our good, but only to trap us in something he can report. I wish you did not trust him or use his support in this affair.

Leave it in God's hands, where it belongs.

—LETTER TO AMBROSIO MARIANO, 1576

God pays the price for those who persevere in prayer. Prayer is the doorway into a treasury of divine gifts. If we shut the door, how can he give us anything? God wants to find the soul alone, empty, and hungry for his love. Why would we seek God's favors when we put obstacles in his way and make no effort to open the door?

I wish I could describe the captivity of my soul in the beginning. I was a prisoner and I knew it, but I didn't understand why. I didn't trust anyone who tried to help me when they said my problems were not serious ones. My spiritual guides recognized my dedication to prayer and thought I was doing well. But inside, I knew better.

I really enjoyed sermons. When someone would preach skillfully and passionately, I could not suppress my warm response. I even listened to bad sermons with eager pleasure. I never grew tired of talking about God or hearing someone else speak about him. Even this bothered me. I was looking for life, and what I was doing was not living, but wrestling with the shadow of death. No one but God could possibly help me, and I could not blame him if he gave up on me.

—LIFE

may 14

The time came when my weary, restless soul discovered health. I was preparing to enter the chapel and noticed a statue loaned to the Incarnation for an approaching festival. It was a representation of the scourging of Christ. It shook me deeply and awakened devotion. I recognized his sacrifice and my lack of gratitude. I began to weep and fell down at his feet, asking him to help me.

At those times, Mary Magdalene was always dear to my heart. During Communion I would frequently ponder her conversion. And I was certain that Christ dwelt within me. Taking comfort, I would kneel at his feet, assured he would never reject my tears. He graciously permitted me to cry. When my awareness of what had brought me to this state began to fade, I would ask Mary Magdalene to intervene for me.

This incident before the statue of Christ's scourging became a deeper, more intense experience. I placed myself unconditionally in God's hands. I promised I would not rise from that position at his feet until he gave me what I sought.

From that moment I began to make spiritual progress.

—LIFE

may 15

•

Some consider themselves to have arrived at such perfection that everyone else seems to have faults. These people are always the ones with the most faults themselves. They of course can't see this and they continue accusing others, wanting to correct what they are already doing well.

The making of new decrees based on such complaints from an individual becomes counterproductive. If we burden people with too many rules, they may neglect some of the more important aspects of the Christian life. This has ruined monasteries and religious orders. Ignoring small matters, they stumble over large ones.

—Visitation

may 16

The way some torment themselves amuses me because they are penitent for no reason. After a few days of penances they begin to think they are doing harm and begin to fear. Then they stop observing the ordinary rules of our life. They abandon even the smallest thing, such as silence, which can harm no one.

A slight headache will sometimes keep us away from choir. We will skip a day because we had a headache in the past, or because we feel one coming on. Then we miss the next three days in order to prepare for any future pains. Inventing our own penances, we perform none at all. The slightest illness gives us permission to ignore our obligations.

Groaning all the time about slight illnesses is a mark of imperfection. If you can survive it, don't talk about it. If you have a serious condition, someone will notice it. Since we live so close together, one complainer will trouble all the others. Worrying aloud is a form of self-indulgence. If your community shares prayer and love, you will always be cared for.

—WAY

may 17

We are ridiculous when we think we can keep the mind quiet and the soul busy simultaneously. It may not be hazardous but certainly wastes our time and energy. It only leads to frustration.

The soul is like the person who is prepared to jump forward and someone suddenly pulls her back. She feels as though she has exhausted all her energy without accomplishing what she planned. When humility is present in anything we do, a sense of frustration never follows.

—LIFE

may 18

Great accomplishments by those who make bold attempts in prayer astonish me. Even a beginner can fly upward to great heights, although, like a young bird with weak wings, weariness may return it to its perch.

I often thought of St. Paul's comment, "I can do all things through him who strengthens me" (Phil. 4:13). I knew I couldn't accomplish anything by myself. This was a very helpful verse, as were the words of St. Augustine's *Confession*: "Give me, Lord, what you command and command what you will." St. Peter lost nothing when he jumped into the sea even though he immediately became afraid and began to sink.

Your first resolutions are important, even though beginners need to be reserved. Seek the wisdom of a spiritual director, but don't get one who wants to teach you to crawl like a toad chasing lizards.

—LIFE

Cross, you are my life's resting place.
You welcome me.
The weakest become strong
Beneath your protective banner.
O life of our death,
Resuscitating us so well.
You have tamed the lion,
You have killed him.
You welcome me.

One who does not love you is a captive
And has no freedom.
You save anyone who turns to you
From evil pathways.
Oh, in this blessed kingdom
Evil has no place.
You welcome me.

—"A la Cruz" (To the Cross)

may 20

·

A wandering mind troubles mental prayer. Without speaking words, we may either make valuable progress or become hopelessly lost. Love will carry a soul a long way, but this kind of advance involves concentrated effort by anyone other than those souls the Lord brings quickly to the Prayer of Quiet.

There are some things that will assist you as you travel a path of silent prayer: a book, a view of meadows, flowers, and water. Creation mirrors the Creator. Such things have quickened my soul and helped me get my thoughts together.

It was not enough for me to try to use my imagination. I am not equipped to visualize things unless I can see them first. I am able to think of Christ, but I cannot picture him. It is as though I am blind or sitting in the dark.

If we are in that kind of darkness but can speak with a person whom we feel beside us, then we are convinced he is truly present. We don't need to see him. This was my personal experience with the Lord, and it explains my fondness for pictures.

—LIFE

I have received a copy of a fresh translation of St. Augustine's *Confession*. The Lord was behind this because I knew nothing about it and had not asked for it. I already had a high regard for St. Augustine because the first convent I entered as a layperson, Our Lady of Grace, belonged to his order. Still, I knew he was as much a sinner as I.

I felt a great kinship with saints who were sinners before God went to work with them. I thought they would be valuable guides. If the Lord could forgive them, I could hope that he would forgive me. To my dismay, many of them responded immediately at the first call of God, while I repeatedly fell away. Thinking of his love gave me courage. I doubted myself, but I never had a doubt about God's mercy.

Reading the *Confession* was like reading the story of my life. When I read his narrative of the child's voice he heard in the garden, it felt as though the Lord was speaking directly to me. Overcome by a weariness I can't express, I wept for a long time.

God help me! A soul suffers when she does not have the freedom to be herself. How did I survive such pain?

—LIFE

may 22

A body is greedy. The more you pamper it, the more it wants. Flesh enjoys any indulgence we grant. The slightest of its appetites, regardless of its importance, grips the poor soul and thwarts its spiritual progress.

Many of the poor have no one to hear their complaints when they are sick. Poverty and self-indulgence are not good companions. Remember that we've not come here to indulge ourselves.

When we begin to subdue these bodies of ours, they give us less trouble. Conquering an enemy like this is one of the grand achievements in life's struggle. You will never be sorry you endured difficulties in order to reach this level of serenity and self-mastery.

—WAY

I recall my first brief, but unmistakable, hints of God. I may have been visualizing Christ within me or reading. Without warning, the presence of God would enfold me in a dramatic and convincing way. This was not at all like a vision—but I think it's called a "mystical experience."

The soul feels suspended outside itself. Love is active, but memory is vacant. The intellect is not lost, but it ceases activity, dumbfounded by the depth of its sudden understanding. God seems to want the mind to know that it is not responsible for this insight.

Previously I often experienced a strong and tender devotion. We can find a little of this through our own efforts. God gives this gift that is a mixture of flesh and spirit. It is possible to enter this state by thinking about our personal insignificance and the overwhelming greatness of God or considering the pain of Christ's passion and the nobility of his being.

We may stumble upon blessings along this path even when we are not looking for them.

—LIFE

may 24

We receive a blessing when we are under orders to do things that demonstrate our lowliness. One day of humble self-knowledge becomes a great favor from the Lord.

The task may be bothersome and cost us more struggles and difficulties than many days of prayer, but the true lover never stops loving and thinks of the Beloved under every circumstance. It would be terrible if the only way we could pray would be to find a quiet corner somewhere.

Of course, it is impossible to sustain many hours of prayer while we busy ourselves with our assigned labor. This doesn't matter. A sorrowful sigh that originates from deep inside us has a powerful effect on our Lord. He understands we regret we have no opportunity to be alone with him in this exile. It is not the length of time we spend praying that brings us benefit.

—FOUNDATIONS

Please try to find out when Jerónimo Gracián receives my letters. I usually write you every time I write him. I received a message today indicating he has not heard from me in a long while. All I do is write. I sent him long letters when I could use the muleteer's services. I hope they have not gone astray because I wouldn't want anyone to get hold of them. If they were lost, that would not be so bad.

Could they be stuck in the chief courier's house down there? I saw them carried away from here. Ask them if they have any of my letters.

All the nuns in Avila are doing well. The letters I am enclosing will confirm this. My brother Lorenzo reports he enjoyed the letters you wrote him. They made him laugh aloud. He shared them with the nuns at St. Joseph's. He will write you because he is very fond of all of you, as I am also.

Stay close to God.

—LETTER TO MARÍA DE SAN JOSÉ, 1576

may 26

When God touches us during the beginning of our spiritual journey, we think this is enough compensation for our service and that nothing more remains. This is true. Even one instance of holy tears is more powerful than anything we can earn with all the trials imaginable. If you have come this far, acknowledge your debt to God. If you do not turn back, God will lead you home.

Avoid false humility. The more we are aware of our spiritual poverty, the richer these gifts will seem. This is a jewel God gives us in love. Our natural response is to love the giver. Prayer growing in the soil of humility yields the fruit of love.

It would have been enough if I had received only one of these spiritual jewels, but the Beloved decided to give me more than I ever would have sought. The Lord gives us this treasure with the obligation that we make good use of it. If we do not respond properly, we will lose it all and become poorer than before.

—LIFE

·

I know people who carefully prepare to receive divine gifts in prayer. I'm not talking about a moment of suspended rapture. If God wants to give such a gift, there is nothing we can do to prevent it from happening. This is a power that takes away our power and lasts but for a brief time.

On the other hand, a quiet prayer may lead to something like a spiritual sleepiness. It overcomes us and we are not sure what to do. This is a challenging subject to write about. I'm not sure I can explain myself.

I know some who may remain in prayer for seven or eight hours, completely absorbed in what they consider to be rapture.[1] They need to be careful. We naturally enjoy pleasure, and if the Lord begins to give pleasure, we want more of it. We can imagine our way into a thousand delightful lies, but we shouldn't allow such pleasure to carry us away.

—FOUNDATIONS

1. Teresa coins new Spanish words to express her thoughts in this section. *Embebecimiento, embobamiento, pasmos, pausada,* and *amortecimientos* may be translated as absorption, stupefaction, dazed, listlessness, and fainting. She uses some of these terms in other works.

may 28

P olice your inner thoughts, especially those concerning rank and honor. "I have seniority." "I did the most labor." "Someone else receives more attention than I do." God forbid that we have ideas like these. When they arise in your mind, suppress them. If you think such thoughts and mention them in your conversation, they will spread like the plague. Ask God to help you avoid this.

You will gain nothing by being concerned about your own honor. Wishing for position and honor robs us of it. Consciousness of rank is poisonous to perfection. This is not a trivial matter. The triggering cause may be slight enough, but you will be tempted to blow it up beyond its significance. If you feel you have been insulted, ask God to give you patience. The devil is working through another person's mouth.

Give no support to anyone who imagines she has been the victim of a snub or insult. That is the kind of pity Job's comforters gave him.

—WAY

Notice how we chant or recite vocal prayer in the choir. We should pray slowly with a soft voice that reflects our manner of life. Chanting with a loud voice is irritating since we are not singing the vocal prayer. It also destroys the calm character of our order. If we fail to emphasize this, some will pray excessively loudly and mitigate the devotion of others.

Let's subdue our voices without any regard for whether or not anyone else thinks it sounds nice. Loud prayers are fashionable today, but we need to stress quietness.

—Visitation

I believe that if a beginner attempts to reach the summit of perfection with God's help, she will not arrive there by herself but will bring many other souls with her. Like the captain of a ship, she will deliver the souls in her care to God. Because the devil will churn up so much chaos along the route, she will need much courage and divine assistance.

The beginning is the most difficult part, although there are crosses to bear all the way to the end. We who follow Christ need to walk his path to avoid getting lost.

—LIFE

may 31

In response to your comments about your personal prayer life, I say the larger the disturbance, the less you need to be concerned about it.

Sometimes there will be a big disturbance from your own weak imagination and bad humor. And then when the devil notices what is happening, he tosses in a little extra. But don't worry about it.

St. Paul says, "God is faithful, and he will not let you be tested beyond your strength, but with the testing he will also provide the way out so that you may be able to endure it" (1 Cor. 10:13).

All of this will be good for you.

Continue taking your medicine and watch your diet. Don't isolate yourself thinking about nothing. Look for some kind of diversion. I wish I could be there with you because I could entertain you with many stories.

—LETTER TO MARÍA BAUTISTA, 1576

june

Because I am a woman and only following orders to write, I hesitate to say what follows. Getting the language of spiritual things correct can be difficult, particularly for an uneducated person like me. Searching for alternative ways of expressing my ideas, I resort to metaphors that may not be appropriate. I will do so now and you may have a good laugh because of my foolishness. I think I read this one somewhere long ago. That forgotten source may have used it to illustrate a different point, but I will use it now for my own purposes.

If you are a beginner, think of yourself as a gardener. You want to plant a garden for the pleasure of your Beloved. The infertile soil in the garden plot is full of weeds. His Majesty cultivates the soil for you, pulling up the weeds, and he gives you some good seed. This happens as soon as you begin a path of prayer and service.

Our task, as gardeners, is to take care of God's plants carefully, watering them so that instead of withering, they may set buds and blossom. The sweet fragrance of these flowers brings pleasure to our Lord. He will visit our garden frequently and enjoy himself among our virtues.

—LIFE

june 2

•

I am surely being foolish and making you laugh as you read, my padre. May God pardon those discalced Carmelite nuns in Seville, those butterflies, who are quietly enjoying what I could not find there. Because of the troubles I had in that place, I envy them. Still, it brings me joy to learn they are taking the meals I suggested to you in an inconspicuous manner.

Those sisters are my joy. You did me a huge favor when you instructed them to write to me with so much to report. You console me by not forgetting me.

I believe that God wants his creation to praise him. We are doing the right thing when we seek to honor and glorify God while not wanting these for ourselves.

His Majesty looks out for us in his own way. Our business is to recognize our lowliness and exalt him the best we can.
—LETTER TO JERÓNIMO GRACIÁN, 1576

june 3

In our monasteries founded in poverty, as well as in those with an income, the apostolic visitator should learn every detail about the diet and treatment of nuns. He should make sure there is provision for their needs, especially the sick. In both kinds of monasteries he should observe their work and make a note of any income from their manual labor. This will encourage those who are working and inspire others to do the same. Enclosed women need recognition for their efforts.

The apostolic visitator should inquire about exceptional gifts. Perhaps there has been some extravagance that will leave the nuns hungry. He can guide them regarding the percentage of income they may use as alms. Budget a reasonable and fixed amount for everything.

The visitator should keep the houses from growing too large, cautioning the nuns against going into debt to construct additions. This does not apply to small projects that cannot do serious harm.

It is better for us to suffer the lack of adequate facilities than to worry about debts and a lack of food.

—VISITATION

june 4

If someone mistreats us, there is no need to complain. We are the great King's brides. Any honorable wife accepts her share of any dishonor done to her husband even though she would rather not. If we want to share in the kingdom of our Spouse Jesus Christ, we must be ready to have our part in his trials and tribulations.

Let the woman who thinks she is the least among us think of herself as the happiest and most fortunate. She will lack no honor either here or in heaven. Let's imitate the humility of the Blessed Virgin.

We live together in a community and this takes care. Our personal honor is not the greatest thing. We harm others with one bad habit more than we help them with many virtues. If any woman cannot endure the customs of our house, she would serve God greatly if she will depart and leave the others in peace. Other convents should hesitate to welcome such a person. A lack of humility is probably behind such behavior.

—WAY

june 5

Rome once gave me permission to establish a convent. Unfortunately, they did not provide any money for it. The whole business gave me a lot of trouble, but when I finished it, there was a sense of accomplishment. I praised the Lord for having used me in such a positive way.

Then I began to think of what I had been through in the process. I could find fault with everything I did. The imperfections of the task were clear. I recalled times of doubt and a lack of faith. The Lord had assured me that all would be well, but I would not let myself absolutely believe it. I wanted to think I could do the job, but sometimes it seemed impossible. Eventually I saw that God had done all the good things and I had made all the mistakes.

So I stopped thinking about it. I have no further need to remember these things. Bless God, who can bring something good out of my poor work! Amen.

—LIFE

june 6

We desire maximum material comfort while attempting to enter heavenly places. But we flutter around like chickens in a pen. We will never find spiritual freedom with this mixture of physical and divine interests. There is a better way.

—LIFE

•

My writing is choppy. I don't seem to know what I'm doing. Read this the best you can, because I am writing the best I can. If it's not good, burn it.

I need to rest some. There are so many things to occupy my time that a week can pass without me putting anything on paper. I lose track of what I am saying. But I should not try to make excuses.

Sometimes I think my self-justifications for my sloppy work make me virtuous. I know better. I hope God will someday give me the humility to remain quiet. Rarely is it helpful to attempt to escape responsibility by excusing ourselves.

A truly humble person will want others to think of them as lowly. Such a person will actually welcome unjust persecution and condemnation. If we want to be like the Lord, there is no better way than this. It doesn't require physical stamina, only God's help.

—WAY

june 8

I will bless God forever! When I abandoned you, you did not abandon me. You remembered me and lifted me up, always holding your hand out to me. Frequently I did not want to take it. I did not even want to notice how often you called me again.

—Life

june 9

Jesus be with you. Please remember to include a small sheet of paper in your messages listing the questions you want me to answer. You write long letters, but they don't seem long because I enjoy reading them so much. It is when I am rushed and have to go back through them to recover your points of interest that they seem lengthy.

Several days ago I wrote you that I would mark two crosses on letters for our padre sent to your address.

When you tell me you understand this arrangement, I will begin doing this.

I'm sorry about your fever. It worries me when you insist you are well. Make sure your menstrual period is not overdue. Don't ignore this. Apply creams and ointments that may lessen the fever, and be sure to tell the doctor. May God make you well.

Give my regards to the others. Their letters are delightful, although I may not have a chance to answer them.
—LETTER TO MARÍA DE SAN JOSÉ, 1576

june 10

O my Lord! If I consider how you suffered unjust accusations, there is not much I can say for myself. It was wrong for me to seek excuses for myself. It is not possible for me to deserve the favors you give me. Why do I want others to think highly of me?

There is no way I can ask you to put up with anything in me that is displeasing in your eyes. Enlighten me. Let me want others to dislike me. You have loved me faithfully, but I often turn away from you.

Reader, there is profit in the confusion you cause your accusers when they see you accept unjust accusations. This will help them more than hearing ten sermons. Try to preach by what you do. Your behavior, both good and bad, will never remain secret. Rejoice when someone finds fault in you. This will be your way to freedom. Eventually, it won't make any difference if they say good things or bad things about you. It will not concern you. The most sensitive of us, with the Lord's help, can gradually gain this freedom.

—WAY

june 11

Absorption and rapture appear to be the same thing, but they are not.

Rapture is a union of all the faculties. It lasts but a brief moment and opens us to great interior enlightenment. Our intellect is not involved. This is the Lord's work.

Absorption is different. While the body is captive, the will is not. Our memory and intellect continue to function, working over matters with "ifs" and "buts." It is better to use our time for something else rather than to remain too long in absorption. Always remember that a loving act is superior to this listless daze.

—FOUNDATIONS

june 12

S ome people believe that devotion will slip away from them if they relax a little. But recreation is good for the soul. We will be stronger when we return to prayer.

There is a time for one thing and a time for another. The soul can become weary of eating the same food over and over again. There is a great variety of food that is wholesome and nutritious. If your spiritual palate becomes familiar with their various tastes, they will sustain the life of your soul, bringing many benefits.

—LIFE

june 13

Your poise and tact while suffering so many defamations of character awakens in me profound devotion mingled with deep grief. I want you to know that God loves you very much and you are truly imitating Christ. Be glad because he is granting your requests for trials. He will reward you.

Regarding that woman, I am convinced this is a work of the devil. He is tempting her to tell these lies about you. He wants to trap you the same way he trapped her. Proceed cautiously and never go to her house. Be sure to put some distance between you.

Sometimes, in this life, it is necessary to be tough. Don't try to fix something that has brewed for four months. Remember that this is a dangerous situation for you. More accusations will only bring more publicity. You know what to do.

—LETTER TO JERÓNIMO GRACIÁN, 1576

Here are the first steps in prayer. I am not aware of any alternatives. If you don't know how to set up a chessboard, you can't play the game. If you don't know how to give check, you will not be able to checkmate. If we play prayer-chess frequently we will checkmate the divine King. He will not be able to move out of our check and will not want to do so.

The queen causes the king the most trouble. The queen that can beat this King is humility. Humility brought him down from heaven into a virgin's womb. Humility will draw him into our souls. He gives even greater humility to the humble person. Humility does not exist without love, and love requires humility. Humility is the first step.

Contemplation is something else. You can spend a brief time daily thinking about your sins and people will call you a great contemplative. You may even think so yourself, but you will be wrong. You did not even know how to set up the chessboard. You thought it was enough to be able to identify the playing pieces. I have been trying to contemplate for twenty years and still lack the ability.

—WAY

june 15

.

Mental prayer is easier than contemplation, but we still need to work hard to achieve it. An absence of the highest values repels the King of Glory. Once in a while, God will snatch a sinful person out of the devil's clutch, and the Lord may entice us with a vision, but he will not raise an evil person to perfect contemplation. Contemplation is a divine union in which the Lord enjoys a soul and a soul enjoys the Lord. The purity of heaven cannot enjoy an unclean soul.

O Lord, how often we force you to wrestle with evil. Why don't we take a lesson from your temptation on the pinnacle of the temple? Instead, we make you struggle every day with uncleanliness. All of our troubles are the result of not giving you our attention. If we looked at the path we are traveling, we would soon get where we are going. Instead, we stumble and fall a thousand times. Our behavior suggests we are not Christians or have never read about your passion.

Spare us from saying, "We're not angels" or "We're not saints" when we sin. We may not be, but we can aspire to be.

Extend your hand to us. We will not be afraid that you may not do your part if we do ours.

—Way

june 16

.

Pay no attention to anyone who tries to dissuade you from your devotions. Of course there are dangers along this way. Even if they attempt to frighten you as you travel the road walked by Christ and his followers, you can be sure they are on a much riskier path. They have no idea what hazards wait for them along their earthly road. They will eventually die of thirst. I advise you not to allow anyone to mislead you by pointing out some other road than the road of prayer.

—Way

june 17

Seek prayer and engage in prayer not for your own pleasure but to gain the strength to serve God. We must be like both Martha and Mary if we are to show true hospitality to the Lord.

You say that you would be glad to bring others to God but that you don't know how to preach and teach. Sometimes the devil gives us grand desires to keep us from getting busy with simple tasks we can perform easily. We overlook a simple task nearby because we think about a great task far away. Instead of doing what is possible, we are pleased to dream about the impossible. Rather than trying to benefit the entire world, concentrate on needs in your own neighborhood.

Don't build castles in the air. The Lord does not look at the greatness of our works, but at the love with which we perform them. If we do what we can, the Lord will increase our ability.

—CASTLE

God does not put us all on the same road. If you think you are traveling the low road, you may be on what God considers the highest. All of us pray, but not all of us will become contemplatives. Contemplation is a gift from God. It is not necessary for our salvation. We may even obtain more merit because we are required to work at it harder.

The Lord will hold for us what we are not able to enjoy in this life. Never be discouraged.

Martha was holy, but we do not know that she was a contemplative. What could be better than to be like her? She was worthy to receive Christ our Lord frequently into her home and prepare meals for him. If she were continually absorbed in devotion the way her sister Mary was, who would cook a meal for this divine Guest?

A community is like Martha's house. All kinds of people live there. Anyone living an active life should not complain about those absorbed in contemplation.

True humility is accepting what the Lord wants you to do. If contemplation, mental and vocal prayer, caring for the

sick, housework, and doing the lowliest chores result in service to the Guest who comes to be with us, what difference does it make which one of these tasks we perform?
—WAY

june 19

Never hesitate to report what is happening. I hear little from other sources. That Padre Gracián writes me at all is remarkable. He is so busy. The letters you report sending to me by way of Madrid, containing information regarding the upheaval that has taken place, never arrived. Most of my letters got through to you except the first pack in which I told you about Gracián's eight-year-old sister, Isabel, receiving the habit and my enjoyable visit with her mother. Other business mail in that package seems to have gone astray. Please confirm this in your next message.

In one of those wandering letters I told you that when I jokingly asked Isabel if she were married, she replied solemnly that she was. I asked her husband's name, and she quickly replied, "Our Lord Jesus Christ."

My detractors' stated reasons for sending me to the Americas amuse me. God forgive them. Perhaps they will say so much so quickly that their rumors will become unbelievable.

—LETTER TO MARÍA DE SAN JOSÉ, 1576

june 20
·

I f you find yourself obsessively thinking about one of the mysteries of the Passion or the glory of heaven, you should try to distract yourself from it. Dwelling repeatedly on a single subject can result in harm from physical weakness or, worse, the imagination.

When a madman throws a fit, he is not in control of himself. He is unreasonable. Something similar could happen to you. Your obsession may be a delightful madness, but it can result in injury.

God is infinite. Why allow just one of his mysteries to hold your soul captive? There is so much about God to occupy our attention. The more of his mysteries we consider, the more he will reveal his grandeurs.

I do not mean that you should think about scattered concepts every hour or every day. This could keep you from enjoying any one of them properly. Don't misunderstand what I am saying about such delicate matters.
—FOUNDATIONS

june 21

My frequent thoughts about God's great goodness are marvelous. Noticing God's remarkable mercy delights my soul. May everyone bless him.

I clearly see how God rewards every good desire, even in this life. Although my own behavior is poor and imperfect, the Lord inspires improvement and values my deeds, hiding my sins. His Majesty has graciously blinded others to my faults, removing my sins from their memory.

God gilds my flaws with gold. He places shining virtues in me, virtually forcing them on me. May God be blessed for putting up with me for such a long time.
—LIFE

june 22

The grace of the Holy Spirit be with you and comfort you in this moment that appears to be one of great loss because of your wife's death. God loves us more than we love ourselves and will help us understand why he permitted my cousin to die. God calls souls when they are most ready to respond.

A long life is not possible. Everything finishes quickly. Your loneliness may not linger if you give yourself over entirely to God. It is a great consolation to know that as she dies, she will live forever. If the Lord takes her to himself now, understand that because she is in the presence of God, there will be help for you and your daughters.

She has been very much in our prayers. And I ask God to lead you to accept his will and recognize how brief the joys and sorrows of this life are.

I'm sending you two melons I found. I wish they were better.

—Letter to Diego de Guzmán y Cepeda, 1576

june 23

Contemplatives are not carrying a lighter burden than others. God lays special crosses upon them. I know from personal experience that God gives contemplatives trials that are unbearable. Only God's encouragement makes it possible for them to survive. God praises them and calls them friends. Few true contemplatives escape these problems. God gives them courage.

Someone living an active life may think contemplatives receive nothing other than God's encouragement. I assure you they suffer more than you realize.

—WAY

june 24

There are two sisters in our monasteries, one a choir nun and the other a lay sister. Both of them pray and are humble and virtuous. They developed an unusually strong desire for Communion, and so they received permission from their confessors to frequently receive. Their affliction grew until it seemed to them that if they did not receive Communion every day they would die. The confessors recognized the agony of their desire and agreed to let them have what they wanted.

That was not the end of it. One of the nuns had such longings that she wanted Communion early in the morning in order to stay alive. This was her honest opinion. She would never lie about such a thing. The prioress wrote me about the matter, saying there was nothing she could do to correct it. By God's grace, I understood what was happening. I remained silent about it until I could be present with them. I didn't want to take the risk of misunderstanding and did not want to contradict someone else's decision.

When I went there I spoke to the confessors and the nuns, giving my reasons for thinking their desire was the product of their imagination. I told them that I had the same desire and would stop receiving Communion in order to convince them they wouldn't have to receive it outside of the regular schedule. I told them all three of us would die. This would be better than to start something in these houses that would cause others who also loved God to want similar special treatment.

I was very strict with them. They were not submitting themselves to obedience, and I could see they were being tempted. They got through their first day with difficulty, and the second day a little better. Their desire gradually diminished. In a few days everyone recognized their compulsion was a temptation, and they were grateful it had been remedied before it got out of hand.

—FOUNDATIONS

june 25

•

Young Isabel is an angel. We praise God for her sweet disposition and happiness. The doctor happened to pass by a room she was in today, an area he doesn't often visit. She tried to run away, but when she knew he had seen her she began to cry. She feared he would ask her to leave, that she probably deserved expulsion from the house.

All of us had a good laugh about this. We love her dearly, and for good reasons.

—LETTER TO JERÓNIMO GRACIÁN, 1576

june 26

I have a lifetime appreciation for the Gospels and discover more recollection in them than in the best books on meditation and prayer. Sometimes we can kill our devotion by studying too many books. Our divine Teacher instructs us patiently and most thoroughly in the pages of the Gospels.
—WAY

june 27

I'm writing this letter so rapidly that it won't be possible for me to tell you everything I want to say. I was obligated to receive a visitor just as I sat down to write. Now it is late at night, and the muleteer will deliver it. Because he is completely trustworthy, I want to state again what I have already sent by other means.

A sixty-year-old childless widow in Aguilar de Campoo (thirteen leagues from Burgos) has been seriously ill and wants to do something good with her estate. She has an income of 600 ducats and a good house and garden. Our founding of monasteries appeals to her, and she is leaving everything to us in her will. She wrote seeking my opinion. Although it is far away, God may still want this done. There are many women there who want to enter even though there is no place for them to go. I will not discourage this widow but tell her I need more information before I could accept it.

Praise God that you have such good health. Be careful what you eat in those monasteries.

May His Majesty watch over you and answer my prayers to make you holy. Amen.

—Letter to Jerónimo Gracián, 1576

june 28

When you receive orders to do a certain job, do it cheerfully. Your active life will bless you.

Other soldiers do their best in their own ways. Sometimes they will need to retreat from great danger, but there is no loss of honor since no one sees them. Captains and the friends of God are always on view. They have a heavy obligation.

We do not understand ourselves and have no idea what to seek. We need to trust God, leaving things in his care. He knows us better than we know ourselves. Humility means we are satisfied with what God gives us. God owes us no favors. He knows we are not able to drink of his cup.
—WAY

june 29

I know of a Bernardine nun who possessed much virtue. Because of her discipline and fasts she grew extremely weak. When she received Communion or got involved with a devotional exercise, she would pass out. She would fall to the floor and remain there for eight or nine hours. She, and those who observed her, thought she was enraptured. This happened frequently and harm would have resulted if no one had a remedy.

Her confessor was my dear friend, and he came to tell me what was happening. I was saddened when I learned about it, because I understood the nature of the phenomenon. I explained it was not rapture but physical weakness. I told him to make her cease fasting and ease up on the disciplines. She obeyed and quickly regained her strength. If it had been rapture, these simple changes would not have made any difference.

Rapture leaves great positive effects in the soul, but her experience left nothing but fatigue.

—Foundations

june 30

I laugh when I read that Friar Juan de Jesús told you I want all of you to go barefoot. I have always opposed this. If he had asked me about it, I would have corrected him. I am trying to attract talented people who might shy away from extreme austerity. The constitution for discalced friars says they may choose either to go barefoot or to wear hemp sandals. This is enough to distinguish us from other Carmelites. I'm sure that sandaled feet will be as cold as bare ones!

I made a similar remark when I said it looked bad for barefoot friars to be riding around on good mules. They don't belong together. Mules are permissible only for lengthy journeys or in an emergency. Some young friars have come here by donkey when they could have walked the short distance easily. It does not look right for barefoot friars to travel on mules and with saddles.

Manual labor is important for all of us, even if it is nothing more than weaving baskets. If there is not enough time, we can do this during the hour for recreation. You know, padre, that I am fond of strictness in the practice of virtue but not in the practice of austerity. This may be because I am not extremely penitential myself.

—LETTER TO AMBROSIO MARIANO, 1576

july

1

We no longer belong to ourselves. We belong to God. When God gives us a desire to cultivate his garden and to be with the Lord of the garden, he grants a blessing beyond our comprehension.

I repeat what I have said many times, returning to one central idea. Never allow your feelings of emptiness or distracting thoughts to upset your soul.

Do you want to be free? Do you want to be calm? Then have no fear of the cross. The Lord will help you carry it. When that happens, you will be pleased with your progress and discover many blessings.

If the well has gone dry, you will not be able to replenish it, but don't stop lowering your bucket.

—LIFE

july 2

Obedience is the fastest and most direct way to reach Christian perfection. This is because we are not the masters of our own will. We must subject it to another.

Often the most reasonable things seems foolish to us. Obedience is like accepting a judge's decision in a difficult case. We tire of arguing and leave the matter to him. Trust the Lord's statement: "Whoever listens to you listens to me" (Lk. 10:16).

The Lord values this kind of surrender. It elevates him to Lord over the free will he has given us. Through surrender, denying ourselves, and struggling against a thousand objections to what seems absurd, we become conformed. He then gives us control over our own desires. Once we are lords over ourselves, we may become perfectly occupied with God. It is like placing a sacrifice on an altar.

We can't give what we do not have. To obtain this treasure we must dig, excavating the mine of obedience. The more we burrow, the more we will find.

—FOUNDATIONS

july 3

•

Your perfectly written letter moves me to praise the Lord, my padre. There is majesty in your words when you write about religious perfection. You comfort my soul. I perceive you are intimate with His Majesty.

I am eager to see more foundations made, trusting God to help the nuns do much good. The enclosed letter will inform you about the one planned for Aguilar de Campoo. The donor is not giving 1,000 ducats, but 600. Perhaps she is holding on to the balance. I have discussed this with Dr. Velázquez because I was hesitant to work against Father General Rossi's will. He asked me to urge Doña Luisa to write the ambassador requesting permission from the father general. He offered all the necessary information, adding that if the father general does not give it, we should seek permission from the pope, pointing out that these houses are mirrors of Spain. I will do this unless you object.

I asked Maestro Ripalda, my good friend who is rector in Burgos, for specific information regarding the transaction of this donation. I told him I would send someone to examine the place and begin negotiations if it seems proper.

Monasteries of nuns really need a leader living among them. The Incarnation Convent has become something for which we can praise God. I wish I could see all of our nuns free of the influence of the friars who wear shoes. I am dedicating my life to enabling us to become an independent province.

It will be a great mercy from God if many prayers could be offered for the church.

—Letter to Jerónimo Gracián, 1576

july 4

Measure your progress by your humility. Progress does not always involve receiving the greatest encouragement when you pray, with many raptures and visions. Such things must wait for heaven. We are to practice the great virtues of humility, sacrifice, and strict obedience.

Why are you in the religious life if you do not want to keep your vows? If you can't do this, you will never be successful in either an active or a contemplative life. Obedience will help you achieve more in one year than you would in many years without it.

—Way

july 5

O my Lord and my God, this verse brings tears to my eyes and deep joy to my soul: "rejoicing in his inhabited world and delighting in the human race" (Prov. 8:31). You want to be with us, present in the sacrament. If we did not prevent it, we could take pleasure in your company and you would be pleased. Imagine! When I hear these words, they always bring great consolation.

Is there a soul anywhere that could return to offending you after it understands this? Yes, I am sure there is one who has done this many times. I am that soul. Lord, please let me be the only one who shows such ingratitude. You are able to produce something valuable even from such an evil. The greater the vice, the more dazzling the wonder of your mercies.
—LIFE

july 6

If anything paralyzes our reason and controls us, we should distrust it. This is not the way to freedom of spirit. It is characteristic of reason that it can find God in everything and then ponder what it means. Anything less than this subjects the spirit, harms the body, and traps the soul. In such an instance, we may compare the soul with a traveler who gets into a swamp or quicksand. All progress ceases. The soul must not only walk, but also be lifted above it by flying. Immobility like this occurs when someone becomes immersed in divinity to the point of suspension.

A few days in this condition are nothing to fear. It is not unusual for weak persons to feel numb for a while. But if it continues beyond a week, it is time to begin looking for a remedy. Discuss it with your superiors.

—FOUNDATIONS

july 7

We can do a lot through our personal efforts that will assist our experience of profound devotion when we begin the spiritual way. Thinking of the glory we desire, the love of Christ, and the miraculous Resurrection will bring us a delight that is spiritual mixed with sensual. These things are good.

Anything that quickens devotion is worthwhile, even if it is a product of mental activity. Still, any devotional blessing we receive is a divine gift and not a reward for our labor. If God has not taken your soul any higher than this, don't strive for more. This will only make spiritual progress more difficult and may result in harm.

You can do many things at this stage to arouse love. Resolve to serve God. There is a book, *The Art of Serving God,* that offers excellent guidance. As long as your mind is still actively participating in your spiritual life, this is good reading.

You can place yourself in the physical presence of Christ, talk with him, laugh with him, and confide in him. Instead of using formal prayers, extemporaneously express your interests. This will result in rapid progress.

If a soul stays in Christ's company it will grow to be intimately in love with him. Rather than letting a lack of burning devotion trouble you, thank God and consciously stay near Jesus, attempting to please him.

—LIFE

july 8

.

I feel that God gave me the grace to realize how much courage it takes to think my way through earthly things, let alone ponder heavenly things.

Many people find it profitable to think about God. Study will greatly assist this practice, provided that humility is the basis of your lessons. I was even recently with some educated men who are showing remarkable progress in prayer.

I am speaking in spiritual terms when I say we should not try to lift ourselves up to God but wait for him to do the lifting. The intellect ceases to function in the mystical experience because God suspends its activity. It is not our responsibility to turn off the mind. If we do that we will become frozen and stupid, achieving nothing. When God takes over our minds he fills them with something astonishing. Without any rational activity, the mind understands more in a moment than it can discover in a lifetime on its own.
—LIFE

If you have an orderly mind and can pray in great solitude, you will benefit from reading some of the books on prayer that have been written by others who are more competent than I. These books take up the mysteries and the passion of the Lord in brief passages for each day of the week. You will find meditations on Judgment Day, on hell, on our own nothingness, and our indebtedness to God. Such books will help you discover your own best method of prayer. You will be on a restful and secure journey.

Others of us are like unbroken wild horses. We are out of control and wander around constantly. Even a skilled rider takes a risk when mounting such an animal. There is always the danger of the horse throwing him out of the saddle. I feel sorry for people like this. They remind me of thirsty people who can see water far away. When they try to get to the water something interrupts their journey at the beginning, in the middle, and near the end. They may defeat the first of these enemies only to confront another. They would rather die of thirst than try to drink such costly water. Their strength fades and their courage fails. Some subdue the first and the second

but surrender to the third, even though the fountain of living water that the Lord promised is only a few steps away.
—WAY

july 10

The Lord said, "Those who drink of the water that I will give them will never be thirsty. The water that I will give will become in them a spring of water gushing up to eternal life" (Jn. 4:14). Words are true when they come from the lips of Truth. The soul will not thirst for anything else in this life, and its thirst for heaven will be greater than any natural thirst on earth. One of God's greatest favors is the satisfaction of our desire for earthly things.

Water does three things. First of all, it has the ability to *cool*. Water refreshes us when we are hot, and it can extinguish a large fire. You will be pleased if you drink God's spiritual water. It will never quench the fire of God's love. This fire becomes your master, setting you free.

Smile when you think of a poor little nun at St. Joseph's gaining mastery over the whole world and all of its elements! With God's help, the saints controlled nature. Fire and water obeyed St. Martin. Birds and fish responded to St. Francis. This is because they succeeded in rejecting the world and subjected themselves to the Lord of the world. They became masters of the world. Earthly water does not affect this fire. An entire ocean of temptation will not keep it from burning.

—WAY

july 11

Second, water also *cleanses.* Water makes it possible to wash things. Christ's living, heavenly, clear water is a potent cleanser. It purifies the soul, washing away every sin. God decides when it is time for us to drink this water of pure contemplation. It is an extraordinary event beyond our control. Unlike earthly water that runs on the ground and becomes cloudy with impurities, this heavenly water is pure and clean. Prayer from mental exercise is not living water. As hard as we try, we cannot free it of the physical influence of our bodies and our fallen nature. We may be meditating on the passing nature of the world, trying to convince ourselves that earthly things are not worth our attention, when we slip

into thinking about all the things here we enjoy. We try to stop, but we go right on thinking about things in the past and in the future. We find it difficult to break out of this cycle of ideas. But when we contemplate, we allow the Lord to take these cares away from us. Our sight is poor and dust from the road blinds us. In contemplation the Lord brings us to our destination without letting us know how it happened.
—WAY

july 12

The third characteristic of water is that it *quenches thirst.* Thirst is a desire for something necessary for life. We die if we have no water to drink, and we drown if we have too much water. My Lord, I desire to plunge into this living water and die in it. That nearly happened once and God alone could help. Since God is the source of the water we need, he accommodates the capacity of the soul to the amount he supplies. God is like a glassblower who expands his goblet until it can contain what he wants to pour into it.

Our desire for living water is insatiable.

But be careful if you face the temptation to overindulge this thirst. It is possible to have too much of a good thing. Cassian told us about a hermit who succumbed to a temptation to jump down a well in order to see God sooner. If such a desire had come from God, it would not have hurt the hermit. God-inspired desires come with insight, moderation, and discretion. Sometimes we even need to stop praying, regardless of the joy it brings. Good judgment applies to everything we do.

—WAY

july 13

You may allow the nuns to begin wearing cheaper, coarser habits in a year. The grumbling will only last a few days after you do this. We don't want those novices to get off to a bad start. This is our first monastery and we want it to be successful.

All of your daughters here are fine, with the exception of those in Beas. They are facing a lawsuit for putting a window in the wall between the monastery and the church that permits them to hear the sermons.

Young Isabel wants to hear from you. I gave her some ice-cold melon. She said it "deafened" her throat. She invents the most delightful expressions. Always a happy child, her gentle disposition reminds me very much of her big brother Jerónimo. May God watch over him even more than he watches over me.

—LETTER TO JERÓNIMO GRACIÁN, 1576

july 14

When the devil misleads us, God will send someone to shine a light on our path. God only needs a few good guides to work with us. If some people think prayer is dangerous, God's servant will show us how good prayer is by her actions as well as her words. If we hear an opinion that frequent communion is not advisable, we may be encouraged by a good guide to participate in it more frequently. With a few good examples, the Lord will regain those the devil has misled. Ignore popular opinion.

Follow those who imitate Christ. Keep your conscience clear. Be humble. Despise worldly things. Trust the teachings of the church. As a result, you will confidently travel an excellent road. There is nothing to fear. Keep the rule that commands you to "pray without ceasing" (1 Thess. 5:17 KJV). If someone urges you to confine your prayers to the spoken kind, ask if your mind and heart should be in what you are saying. When they answer, "Yes," they are agreeing there is no way you can avoid mental prayer and contemplation.

—WAY

july 15

I am personally familiar with temptations that beginners experience. Here is my best advice: when you begin the spiritual path, try to be cheerful and relaxed. Devotion does not require the opposite.

Also while you need to be careful to guard against the foibles of human nature, you should also enjoy times of recreation. When you return to prayer, you will take a refreshed spirit.

Approach prayer confidently. Keep no secret desires. Trust God's power. With God's help you will gradually approach the place where the saints stood. They had to apply themselves with determination and accept small advances. God welcomes courageous souls if they are not arrogant. I have never seen such a soul falling behind. On the other hand, cowardly souls hiding behind false humility make scant progress.

—LIFE

july 16

We need to use discretion regarding which actions of the saints we imitate and which we merely admire. It would be wrong for someone who is weak or sick to begin fasting, or do rough penances, or head for the desert where there is nothing to eat and sleep would be difficult. Austerities like this are not for such a person.

God will help us to grow free of the world, disregard personal honor, and let go of our possessions. We fear the earth would collapse beneath our feet if we turn our attention away from physical things for a moment of spirituality.

The slightest thing will give us the greatest trouble when we have not made much spiritual progress. And we call ourselves spiritual!

We can imitate the saints by seeking solitude and silence. This will never injure our bodies. Do not believe the temptation that spiritual practices may kill us or destroy our health. Tears will not make us blind. I have been sickly all my life. My body has often kept me from active devotion. Satan tried to convince me that I was ruining my health and suggested I get some rest. I told him I did not want rest, but the Cross.

My health has improved since I stopped worrying about my ease and comfort. Don't be frightened by your own thoughts when you begin to pray. Trust me. I have been there. Perhaps the story of my failures may help as a warning to others.

—LIFE

july 17

If you enjoy thinking things through with your mind, don't spend all of your time that way. Intellectual activity is valuable and can assist our prayers, but the mind needs an occasional Sabbath of rest. It may seem like a waste of time to you, but I tell you the loss is your greatest gain.

The thing to do is to place yourself in the presence of Christ and, without worrying about the details, simply talk with him. Enjoy his companionship. Tell him what you need and thank him for permitting you to be with him.

Sometimes we need to cogitate, but this time all we need is to be there in his presence. Instead of our palate growing dull by repetition, we can enjoy a variety of spiritual foods.
—Life

july 18

God will not stop anyone coming to drink his living water. Neither does he insist that some travel one way and others another. God's mercy is great, but he forces no one to drink. He gives us the ability to follow and to drink in many ways. Numerous streams flow from this abundant spring. Some are large and some are small. There are wading pools for faithful children. We will never lack the water we need to quench our thirst.

Push on. The only reason you are here is to keep striving. It is better to die than to miss this water. The Lord may keep you a little thirsty through this life, but you need not fear that he will fail to give you what you need. Let us never fail him.

—WAY

july 19

While I was in a rapturous state I received a vision from the Lord. I saw the bodily form of an angel standing near my left side, a rare event for me. Usually the angels I see are only an intellectual vision not involving my eyes.

The angel was small and beautiful with a face that burned with fire. They never tell me their names, but angels are distinctive individuals in a way I am not able to explain. He held a long golden spear with a flaming iron point. He thrust it into my heart repeatedly, piercing my entrails. When he withdrew it, he seemed to pull them out also, leaving me on fire with great love of God. The great pain caused me to moan, but the pain was so sweet I did not want it to stop. This was not a physical pain but a spiritual pain, although the body is greatly involved. It is a caressing of love between the soul and God.

I was beside myself during the days this lingered. I did not want to speak with anyone. All I wanted to do was to embrace my pain, which is pure joy.

—LIFE

july 20

You are on the royal road to heaven along which you will gather precious treasure. But it should be no surprise that you travel at a high cost. I can assure you the prize that awaits you at the end will far exceed any difficulties you may be having now. Resolve not to stop until you drink Christ's living water. It will be more than worth the effort.

Many will try to discourage you. They will tell you it is enough to say the Lord's Prayer and Ave Maria. I agree with that. It is enough. But let your own prayers spring from the one our Lord himself spoke. If our devotion were not so weak, we would not need any other prayers or methods of prayer.

—WAY

july 21

The favors God is granting you amaze me. I think it is good for you to desire devotion. There is a difference between desiring devotion and asking for it. What you are doing is best. Leave the matter entirely in God's hands. He knows what is best. Keep trying to travel along the path I described in my letter.

If you wake up in the night with impulses of God's love, it would not be bad to sit up in bed for a while, but be sure to get enough sleep. If you deny yourself sleep you may become unable to pray.

And don't let yourself get chilly. Cold is not good for the pains you are experiencing in your side. Why do you want terrors and fears? God's love is leading you. The devil is not the only one who inhibits prayer. Sometimes a merciful God takes prayer away from us, and this may be a greater favor than giving us much prayer. Any prayer God gives you is much better than contemplating hell, which you wouldn't be able to do if you wanted. Since there is no reason for it, don't desire it.

I picked up your letter and read it again. I missed the fact that you want to get out of bed at night. I thought you merely wanted to sit up in bed. That seemed to me to be a lot because it is important not to skimp on sleep. Absolutely do not get up, regardless of how much fervor you may feel. Do not be afraid of sleep.

—LETTER TO LORENZO DE CEPEDA, 1577

july 22

Ponder a moment from Christ's passion such as when they tied him to the pillar. Your mind may try to find reasons why he had to suffer so much pain and agony. You struggle to grasp his loneliness and isolation. If you spend time studying these questions, you can gather much understanding from the effort. All of us should begin, prolong, and end with this method of prayer. It is an excellent and safe method to use until the Lord leads us in more supernatural paths.

Still, some of us are better equipped to meditate on something other than Christ's passion. As heaven has "many dwelling places" (Jn. 14:2), many roads also lead there. A few find meditation on hell to be a valuable exercise. Others meditate on death. There are those who are too sensitive to linger with passion imagery. They prefer to consider the power and glory of God revealed in his creation, reflecting upon his infinite love. This latter way is very good, but we need to balance it with specific thoughts about Christ's life, remembering what he did for us. He is the source of everything good, past and present.

—LIFE

july 23

.

Seek wise counsel. An experienced guide is essential. If your spiritual director has limited personal experience, serious mistakes will result. Such a person can quickly lead you astray because he will not understand what he is trying to help you understand. Beginners usually find the experience of having a guide exciting and tend to accept all of their instruction without question.

I know people who have received great injury by advice from inexperienced spiritual guides. I feel sorry for ones such as the woman who can no longer make up her own mind about prayer. Ignorant spiritual directors can harm both the soul and the body. With their lack of knowledge about spirituality they can impede progress in prayer. One woman told me her guide refused to allow her to explore beyond self-knowledge for eight years. Since the Beloved had already led her to the Prayer of Quiet, this leash tortured her.

It is important, then, to have a relationship with a knowledgeable guide who has good judgment and personal experience with matters of the spirit. Formal education is helpful, but not required. You can always find someone with an education to answer your theological questions, but unless he practices prayer himself, all of his learning will be of no help to a beginner on this path. Learning is a wonderful thing that allows another to teach us out of our ignorance. We need exposure to the truths of sacred Scripture. God save us from foolish devotions!

—LIFE

july 24

One does not need to choose between mental prayer and spoken prayer. Both are important. Should anyone tell you prayer is hazardous, that person is your chief danger. Avoid such company. There is never a risk in prayer. Any fear of it comes from the devil who has cleverly trapped some who pray.

The world can't see clearly. It does not think of the thousands who fell into heresies and other sins when they gave in to distractions instead of practicing prayer. A few of these who fell away were in fact seduced as they prayed. This is Satan's way of frightening others and discouraging virtuous actions. Be careful not to run away from something good with an idea that you are saving yourself.

—WAY

july 25

Practicing mental prayer is not dependent upon keeping your mouth shut. Vocal prayer and mental prayer blend when we are conscious of the fact that we are speaking with God. It is possible to recite the Lord's Prayer while thinking about other things. But when we speak with such a great Lord, we need to remember who is listening and speak with appropriate respect. It is not enough to praise the Lord with our lips alone.

Mental prayer and spoken prayer are partners. If we remember who we are when we pray, and the majesty of God who is listening to us, there is no way we can even begin to say anything without first engaging in profound mental prayer. We do not approach and speak to a prince as casually as we talk with a peasant.

God's humility permits us to enter his presence and to speak with him. He doesn't command the guards to throw us out. Angels in God's presence know their King prefers the unskilled language of a humble peasant to the speech of the wisest and most educated if they lack humility. His goodness is no excuse for rudeness on our part.

When you approach God, remember who is going to hear you, and think about the majesty of God while you pray.

—Way

Prayer for beginners is like drawing water up from a well. Our own muscles are responsible for the water that irrigates our garden. The next step is to allow the garden master to show us a more efficient way. He will turn a waterwheel, using natural forces to deliver water through aqueducts, producing more water with less expenditure of effort. Instead of working constantly, the soul may take a little rest. This is an illustration of the Prayer of Quiet.

In a Prayer of Quiet the soul begins to come together in a state of interior recollection. This has a supernatural aspect because it could never accomplish this on its own. Although we may have become tired pulling up water, using our understanding to fill the buckets, the water of this second degree is higher and easier to obtain.

What happens is a gathering together of the soul's faculties, permitting the soul to taste more of prayer's sweetness. The faculties are neither lost nor sleeping, but one's will becomes occupied to the point of captivity, agreeing to become a prisoner of God. "For the love of Christ urges us on" (2 Cor. 5:14). We consent to this without hesitation.

O my Lord Jesus! Your love in this place is precious to us. You hold us so closely we are not able to love anything else but you!

—LIFE

july 27

Sometimes when your will is united with God, your other faculties may intrude. Ignore them if that happens. Continue basking in joy and peace. In response, your faculties will act like unhappy doves that are displeased with the food freely offered them. They fly off looking for something better. When they find food scarce out in wild areas they return to the feeder. Wandering faculties come back to discover what your personal will is enjoying so much. If the Lord tosses them a handful of food they will settle down and eat. Otherwise they keep looking. The soul gains nothing by attempting to force the faculties of memory and imagination to paint a picture of what it is enjoying.

This second state of prayer is a great consolation to the soul. It may linger for a long time, but it is not as fatiguing as attempting to draw water from a well. At this point, the soul rises above misery and glimpses glory. God becomes the source of all virtues. Cravings for commonplace things diminish. Neither wealth, nor power, nor honor, nor pleasure come close to comparison with this happiness.

—LIFE

july 28

A new arrival at this second level of prayer may be confused. If God is guiding her along the path of fear that I experienced, the confusion will be painful. It is particularly exasperating if she can't find anyone who understands what is happening. For this reason, it can be an incredible relief to find your experience described in a book.

I lost a lot of time because I did not know how to continue this journey. It is agonizing to arrive here alone. Many of the books I have read about spiritual matters do not explain things clearly. I beg the Lord to help me help you through these words. I wish I had more time to work on this, but I am living in a house that I recently founded. Community relations and the business of the world hound me. I write in short bursts, never able to settle into it deeply. With the Lord's inspiration, the writing flows easily. When inspiration evades me, nothing I write makes any sense despite my years of experience. I try to pray as I write. Sometimes I wonder how I have produced anything at all.

—LIFE

july 29

Come back with me now to our garden. Notice the buds are swelling on the fruit trees. Soon they will burst into bloom and set fruit. Take a deep breath and smell the fragrance of carnations and other flowers.

Such imagery charms me. The idea of the soul as a garden where the Beloved takes walks has always appealed to me. As I began taking this path, I begged His Majesty to make the perfumes of little flowers of virtue more intense for me. I could sense they were beginning to blossom inside me. I did not seek this for myself, but for his glory. I gave

God permission to cut flowers as he pleased, understanding that pruning would cause greater growth.

I mention pruning because sometimes the soul neglects this garden. It turns dry and irrigation becomes a challenge. The soul is not able to find a single virtue in the garden God placed in her care. She feels like a failure.

The Lord works through this spiritual aridity. If the "gardener" will relinquish her personal importance, God will take over the cultivation, pulling up weeds and grooming valuable plants. She must recognize that if God denies his rain of grace, there is nothing she can do about it. Her greatest effort will not keep this garden alive. She is impotent. But when she responds in humility, flowers will once again return.

—LIFE

july 30

It is not enough to be able to repeat the words of the Lord's Prayer without understanding what they mean. We need to understand who "Our Father" is and to know the Lord who teaches us this prayer. God forbid that we fail to think of our Lord when we repeat this prayer!

Remember that Christ recommends that we pray in private, the way he often prayed alone. We can't speak to God and the world simultaneously. How can we try to pray while listening to people talking or letting our uncontrolled minds wander? Circumstances sometimes prevent undivided attention to prayer. God may allow us to suffer this for days at a time. But don't worry about it. This is not your fault. Above all else, pray the best you can.

Do you think God is silent because you cannot hear him? He will speak clearly to your heart when you sincerely ask him to do so.

—WAY

july 31

Jesus be with you. The sardines you sent arrived without spoiling, and the sweets also came at a good time. I wish you had kept the best for yourself. Please don't send anything else unless I ask for it.

For the past eight days I have been in a condition that, if it continues, will keep me from dealing with all the business demanding my attention. I've started having raptures again. They distress me when they happen in public. One occurred during Matins. Resisting does not help, and I can't hide them. They embarrass me. Pray that God will spare me these raptures. They do not seem to improve my prayer. It's almost as though I were slightly inebriated.

Before this began about a week ago, I suffered spiritual dryness. But I am probably reporting too much. Nothing more should be written or spoken about it.

Regarding your own experiences, I have no comment. They are certainly beyond your understanding and are the beginning of many blessings if you do not carelessly lose them. I have had similar experiences. Good rest and good work for God followed them.

The physical reactions you mention are temporary and of no importance. They have nothing to do with the quality of your prayer. You say that you feel as if nothing happened when it is over. St. Augustine says God's spirit passes without leaving a trace, the way an arrow travels through the air. Sometimes the condition will linger. It's like being able to feel the sun even when it is behind clouds. The soul feels settled far away, animating the body without being in it.

—LETTER TO LORENZO DE CEPEDA, 1577

august

1

The road that leads to God does not seem narrow to me. We travel a broad, safe highway rather than a path. I see the mountain passes of sin, with their treacherous rocks, far in the distance. We travel a narrow path along a knife-edge with cliffs and traps, which is risky for a careless traveler. But the one who loves God walks safely on a wide and royal road.

Stumbling once in a while is not a problem because God reaches out to help. I cannot imagine the insecurity of following the crowd. We find true safety when we attempt to travel God's road.

—Life

august 2

A married couple reflects each other's mood. If one is happy, the other is happy. If one is sad, the other is sad. The Lord offers us the same kind of relationship. When your emotions are elevated, look upon the bright and beautiful risen Lord. He is majestic, triumphant, and wonderful. When you are downhearted, see him going to the Garden of Gethsemane. "I am deeply grieved, even to death" (Matt. 26:38). Or look at him crucified because of his great love for you. Imagine him struggling, carrying the weight of the cross. Comforting your grief, he will forget his own. Now the compassion you feel does not need formal prayer language. "If you suffer this much for me, what can I suffer for you? How can I have any complaints?"

You want to know how you can do this. You say, "If I had been with him then I could have looked." I doubt it. You would not likely have gone to stand at the foot of the cross with the women. They were not among a courteous and civil crowd.

Christ will tell you what to say. If you can converse with people here, you should have no trouble talking with God.

Linger at the good Master's side. Concentrate on learning his lessons. He wants you as his disciple and he will never leave you unless you leave him.

—WAY

august 3

I am not asking you to involve your mental faculties for extended and clever meditation. Simply look at Christ. Nothing can keep you from focusing your soul's attention on your Lord. If you can look at ugliness, you can look at unimaginable beauty.

Jesus never takes his eyes off you. He has endured thousands of sins against him, but these have not discouraged him. He waits for you to look his way. If you seek him, you will find him.

—WAY

august 4

A serene satisfaction accompanies the deeper level of prayer known as the Prayer of Quiet. One experiences a sense of deep satisfaction and calm, a gentle happiness. When this is as far as you have come in prayer, you will think there is nothing beyond it. You will not want to do anything to disturb such a moment. You may even hold your breath. As there was nothing you could do to arrive here, there is also nothing you can do to remain longer than the Lord wants you to be in this state.

Your faculties do not cease to operate in this quiet stillness when everything in your soul comes together, but you will be content to linger in God's presence. As long as this recollection continues, the calmness remains. Even though your perception of other things remains busy, your will is united with God. Your mind and memory will gradually submit to the tranquility. Nothing can detract from this experience. This spark of love for God continues to glow.

I beg God to help me explain this clearly. Many souls arrive at this state, but only a few continue higher. I don't know why.

—LIFE

Enormous dignity comes to the soul in the Prayer of Quiet. You begin to recognize you no longer exclusively belong to physical reality. You are becoming familiar with heaven, provided you do not interfere with God's activity. If you turn back now, you will sink all the way to the bottom. God rescued me from such a fall.

If you experience the Prayer of Quiet, know yourself. Seek a humble and holy confidence in yourself. Without self-confidence you will return as a slave to Egypt. All of us are human. We all need to guard against sin even after receiving these favors from God. I urge you, no matter what, to keep praying. If you abandon prayer, you are taking a great risk.

—LIFE

august 6

During the Prayer of Quiet, your will may be united tranquilly with the divine as your mind continues to ramble without purpose. It is better to ignore the intellect than to pursue it. Remain under control like a practical bee while you enjoy God's gift. If the bees buzzed around trying to herd all the others into the hive, there would be no bees inside carrying out the important job of making honey.

You need to be careful about this. Don't search for reasons or start organizing your thoughts. There is no explanation for what is happening beyond the goodness of God. With an awareness of your nearness to God, pray for the church, for those who have asked for your prayers, and for the dead. You will not need to use noisy words.

This kind of simple prayer contains more than a multiplicity of ideas generated by your mind. Your love will increase. By placing a little straw of humility on this glowing fire, you will cause it to burst into flame more readily than you could with a great load of the logs of reason. In fact, scholarship will quickly extinguish it.

—LIFE

W hat I have said is valuable advice for the educated men who ordered me to write, as well as for everyone else who may come to this condition of prayer. Perhaps you may begin to apply familiar passages of Scripture to this spiritual experience. Although your education will certainly be helpful before and after you pray, I think there is little need for it during the actual time of prayer. Its function would be to dampen the flame.

Because of our close proximity to the light, we will see with an astounding clarity. For me, it is as though I become another person. I understand very little of what I read in Latin, particularly the Psalms, but in the Prayer of Quiet I comprehend the Latin as though it were Spanish. I even begin to enjoy a meaning in the language that goes beyond the words.

Now there are certainly times when educated people must preach or teach. It is their responsibility to use their learning to help others like me. This is ministry to souls when they dedicate such teaching to God.

And yet, when we are near Infinite Wisdom, a single act of humility is worth more than all the science in the world.

This quietude is not a time for scholarly discussion but for understanding ourselves and presenting ourselves humbly before God. Be willing to seem foolish here.

—LIFE

august 8

Our Father in heaven" (Matt. 6:9). What a way to *begin* a prayer, O Lord. A favor this great belongs at the end. As we start to pray you fill our hands with so much. How can we say another word? This is enough to contemplate right here. Our soul can rise above itself, allowing the holy Son to reveal the beauty of heaven where our Father lives.

O Lord, you give us so much with your first word. You humble yourself to become one of us. All of us become God's children. He cares for us and forgives us like a good parent. God loves us.

The location of heaven is not important. God is everywhere. Wherever God is, there is heaven. If our Lord is present, there is completeness of glory. Saint Augustine looked for God in many places only to discover God within himself. Understand this truth. You do not need to travel to heaven in order to speak with God, and neither do you need to call out loudly. He is near, and he will hear the quietest whisper. There is no need for wings. All you need is a place where you can be alone and look inside yourself.

We may talk with God as we would with a parent, asking for what we need, reporting our troubles, and expressing our unworthiness.

—WAY

august 9

Become familiar with saying the Lord's Prayer in a recollected way. You will find this very profitable, as it will keep you focused and restlessness will not disturb you. Eventually, you will no longer need to seek God. You will have God within you.

Until I learned to pray this way, my prayer life was unsatisfactory. Keep practicing this way and you will gradually master yourself. As you pray, you can listen to God within you. You will never need to pull away from God's companionship.

You may practice recollection frequently during the day. The more you do this, the more you will discover its benefits. Once the Lord grants it, you will not be willing to trade it for any other treasure.

If you pray in this manner for about a year, God will help you arrive at a new level of spirituality, providing you with a solid foundation in a relatively short time.

—WAY

august 10

Our good Jesus tells us to ask for specific things in prayer. Couldn't he instead have ended the Lord's Prayer quickly by saying, "Father, give us what is good?" When we speak with an omniscient God, there should be no need to say more than this. In the Garden of Gethsemane Jesus placed himself in his Father's hands. "Father, if you are willing, remove this cup from me; yet, not my will, but yours be done" (Lk. 22:42).

We are not as resigned to God's will as Jesus was. He needs to teach us to ask for things we want in order to give us time to reflect on their value. We may not receive precisely what we request, but something better. This may leave us disappointed because we do not think we are rich unless we have cash in our hands.

If the Eternal Father gives something to you, do not throw it back in his face. Consider your requests carefully. If you think it may not be valuable, don't ask for it. Ask the Lord to inspire your requests. Sometimes we come to see that we have an appetite for unhealthy food.

—WAY

august 11

•

My illness will probably serve a good purpose because I am adjusting to letting a secretary take care of some of my writing. I should have been doing this previously in dealing with minor matters. I took some pills and I am feeling much better now. My headache has greatly diminished. I probably should not have been fasting. I was almost incapacitated and could not pray, but don't worry about me. I am taking good care of myself.

I want to be well again to keep from being a burden. I am not able to digest mutton and must eat fowl. The fasting

I did while continuing to do hard work was not a good idea for someone approaching sixty-two. This body of mine has always been a handicap.

The hair shirt I sent you is too coarse. Don't wear it, and don't feel imperfect because you find it disagreeable. This is not important. I am sending you another one that you can wear two days a week. Take it off before you go to bed. If it is too tight around your waist, put some soft linen between the hair shirt and your stomach. If you feel any irritation around your kidneys, stop this discipline immediately. God wants your health more than your penance. "To obey is better than sacrifice, and to heed than the fat of rams" (1 Sam. 15:22).

—LETTER TO LORENZO DE CEPEDA, 1577

august 12

•

The third source of water that irrigates the garden of the soul is that which flows through a stream or from a spring. This one does not require as much labor as cranking a waterwheel or pulling up a bucket from a well. We still need to maintain the water channel, but the Lord provides most of what we need.

Prayer on this level greatly reduces our need for our faculties. The soul's delight grows in intensity. The experience is a kind of death—a dying to earthly things and a dying into God.

I can't find the words to describe what happens to the soul. She wonders if she should speak or remain silent, laugh or weep. It is a glorious mystification, a spiritual madness. It is a blessed craziness containing all wisdom.

I experienced this five or six years ago. I never understood it and I couldn't explain it. I decided that when I came to this part of my story I would say little or nothing about it. It was clear to me that this was not the union of all the faculties, but it was higher than any previous state of prayer. I didn't know what to say about it.

—LIFE

august 13

·

You demonstrated true humility when you ordered a simple person like me to write this. Maybe that's why the Lord gave me the gift of this third level of prayer today following Communion. I was busy thanking God when His

Majesty interrupted me by offering some metaphors I could use to explain this infused quiet. I instantly understood what to say. At last, praise God, I think I will be able to communicate.

The soul's flowers begin to bloom and spread their fragrance. It wants others to join it in praising God and participating in this joy. It's almost too much for one person. It is like the woman in Christ's parable who searched for a lost coin and cried out, "Rejoice with me, for I have found the coin that I had lost" (Lk. 15:9). David must have felt the same way when he played his harp and sang praises to God.

God help me. In this condition a soul wants nothing but tongues with which to praise God. She jabbers a thousand holy follies. I have done this while expressing my experiences in emotional stanzas even though I am not a poet.

—LIFE

august 14
•

I n the Prayer of Quiet, the Lord begins to assure us he is actively responding to our requests. He gives us a taste of his heavenly kingdom while we remain on earth. This is a divine gift. There is nothing we can do to achieve this. Our awareness of the Lord's presence brings peace to our soul. We understand we are extraordinarily near union with God.

This experience is similar to Simeon's when he took the infant Jesus in his arms at the temple. "My eyes have seen your salvation" (Lk. 2:30). Simeon saw nothing more than a poor couple's baby, but God revealed much more than that to the righteous old man. In the same way, although not as clearly, the soul perceives it is near the end of its journey.

The body remains motionless. One does not dare to move. Speaking becomes a bother. In such a state praying the Lord's Prayer may take an hour. In the palace and near the King, we may cry. One's only desire is to praise God.

This state may continue for two days if we become busy with ministry. We have a great capacity for service to God after the Prayer of Quiet. We may combine the active with the contemplative life. At times such as these, the Martha and the Mary in us work together.
—Way

august 15

W hen people experience the pleasure of the Prayer of Quiet, they sometimes wish they could prolong it by methods such as holding their breath. Controlling this prayer is as impossible as stopping sunrise and sunset. It is a divine gift far beyond our ability. There is nothing we can do to increase or diminish it. All we can do is admit we are not worthy of it and give thanks to God with few words and an upward gazing.

To make room for the Lord and allow him to accomplish his work in us, we may try to find greater privacy. We may limit our speech to single words, the way we might puff a candle to encourage its flame to return. Long speeches are counterproductive.

When you reach this state of prayer, your understanding may wander off looking for worldly things. Laugh at it for being so silly. Remain quiet. Let your thoughts come and go without trying to manage them. If we try to take control of everything, we will lose everything.

—WAY

august 16

Imagine that God is teaching his short prayer to you personally. The Master is near you. You do not need to shout because he is beside you. If you want to pray the Lord's Prayer, remain beside the one who taught it to you.

"Ah!" you say. "This is meditation and I don't know how to do that. All I want is to pray a vocal prayer." Yes, I have described mental prayer in relation to the Lord's Prayer. It is impossible to recite it faithfully without an awareness of God. May God help you patiently focus on Christ and spare you irrelevant thoughts as you pray.

—WAY

august 17

Every degree of prayer I have previously described involves the soul as a gardener. In the ultimate state of prayer, we rise above our ordinary senses. The experience of goodness defies understanding and explanation. In the earlier levels of prayer, our faculties continue to function, but in this fourth kind of "water" both body and soul lose their service. Everything about it draws into a delightful, indescribable union.

I have no idea how to explain this prayer. I lack the language of mystical theology. I am not able to understand the distinctions between soul, mind, and spirit. All three seem to be one to me, although I know the soul may jump out of itself the way a coal bursts into flame, increasing violently until it ascends high above the fuel. That does not make the fire a different thing. It remains the same flame of the same fire.

Because you are educated you may understand all of this. I have nothing else to say about it.

I always prefer, instead, to discuss a personal experience of this union with the divine. Union occurs when two distinct things become one.

—LIFE

august 18

Divine love elevates the spirit in union. The elevation is not the same as the union itself. When iron gradually turns red hot in a fire, it loses its ordinary nature. I am trying to describe personal experience. Putting this on paper feels like trying to write Greek.

Because of the difficulty of writing as my superiors ordered me to do, I put my pen down and went to Communion. I know that our Lord shows mercy to the ignorant, and obedience is an enabling virtue. God has now enlightened my understanding, giving me the vocabulary I need and the ability to use these words. Anything worthwhile I write comes from God, even though the mistakes are always mine.

Our Lord oversees the little bird of a soul that is advancing through the steps of prayer until he can give it rest in its nest. He watched as it fluttered on its wings of understanding and will, seeking God and trying to please him. Now he enjoys rewarding her, and what a reward it is! No price is too high.

—LIFE

august 19

The soul remains conscious while approaching union with God, but it becomes woozy with excessive joy. Bodily senses cease to function. I can report that this kind of prayer has never harmed me, even when I was ill when it happened. I always felt better when it ended.

My first experiences with the Prayer of Union were brief. It seemed as though the great brightness of the sun melted the soul. A half hour would seem lengthy for such entrancement. I think it has never lasted that long, but there is no perception of the passage of time. Eventually some human faculties recover and begin to pester one's will. The will may control them for a while, only to have them wake up again.

With this kind of give and take, several hours may pass in prayer. When our faculties become intoxicated with this heady divine wine, they quickly yield to our will, but this state of total absorption lasts only a short time. Our physical faculties need a few hours to adjust when the prayer has ended.

Now I must describe the indescribable. When I left my writing and attended Communion, I experienced the Prayer of Union. As I pondered the difficulty of putting anything about it on paper, the Lord said this to me: "My daughter, the soul utterly melts, permitting it to give itself more and more to me. I live in it. Because it cannot comprehend what it understands, it understands by not understanding."

That's the only way I can express it. God unites with the soul!

—Life

•

Comprehending that the fruits of prayer are not our own, we want to share them with others. We can give them away without any loss. No one wants to be the only soul so rich. Companions may then notice the fragrance of these flowers and become eager to approach them. They see the fruit and desire a taste of it.

When this garden's soil is well cultivated by persecution, distractions, illness, and a loss of self-interest, it will accept enough water to prevent it ever becoming parched again. On the other hand, if the dirt is a wasteland covered with thorns, the way mine was in the beginning, it will soon be dry again. Unless the Lord kindly sends rain, the careless gardener's plot is lost. The Lord has startled me by sending such showers.

My superiors ordered me to write this for the comfort of others who are weak like me. If you have started to give yourself to prayer, never be discouraged. Trust the power of God.

—LIFE

august 21

Many who did not realize my shortcomings began to express a good opinion of me. Others were critical of me. I agreed with these second ones and never considered them my enemies.

I asked you, O God, to notice how right my critics were. They said, "She wants to become a saint." "She's inventing novelties before she fully observes her own rule." "Other nuns in her house are better." "She's introducing negative, evil ideas." They spoke the truth and, as a result, became my instructors.

As this persecution continued, I read a psalm. "You are righteous, O Lord, and your judgments are right" (Ps. 119:137). I realized how true this is. I have never been tempted to doubt God's goodness. I held on to my faith and my devotion grew.

Then I began to wonder why you would allow so many of your faithful servants to remain unaware of the blessings you gave me, as undeserving as I am. You answered me clearly. "Serve me instead of meddling with these things." I was terrified because this was the first time I had ever heard you speak.

—LIFE

august 22
•

O my Lord, you are good. Let all creatures praise you forever. You have loved us so much we can begin to express the nature of this communication you have with souls in exile. Why do you give such high ability to souls who are great sinners? I can hardly understand it.

How can I continue without retreating? I may relieve myself by saying foolish things. I am a wicked woman. My talents are not only hidden but also buried, committed to vile earth. Someone else could do a better job of writing this than I. Lord, use what I say to benefit those who read it.
—Life

august 23
•

Y our will be done, on earth as it is in heaven" (Matt. 6:10). When our Lord finds a soul who greatly loves him, he knows that soul can suffer a lot for him. Our degree of love determines our ability to bear crosses. If you have great love, your prayers need to be more than polite words.

Be ready for whatever the Lord requires of you. If you place conditions on your love, you are offering him a jewel and then pulling it away before he can accept it.

Mockery in prayer is no way to treat our Lord who suffered so much for us. Since we pray the Lord's Prayer frequently, we are often in danger of teasing him. Go ahead and give him the jewel. He gave it to you in the first place, and now you can return it.

"Your will be done" means you are asking him to do whatever he desires. It is as though you have prayed, "If you want me to suffer trials, give me strength and let trials come to me. If you are allowing illness or poverty, I will not turn away from you. Treat me as your own, as you please."

—WAY

august 24

Look into your own heart. Attempt to stay with our Lord as you pray. He will not hide from you, but will make himself known to the degree that you desire.

If we wander away from Christ, looking for earthly things in prayer, what can he do? He will not drag us back against our will.

Being near God as we pray is like approaching a fire. The fire may be large, but if we keep our distance it will only warm us a little. A properly prepared soul draws near God intending to drive the cold away, and it will absorb and retain warmth. If a spark leaps out, it will ignite the soul.
—WAY

august 25

Ignore any slights you may receive. If you insist on fine points of honor, you are a child building a straw house. You do not understand the nature of honor. You are like so many others who are easily hurt. The world teaches us that we profit if we can possess its honor. This isn't true. The soul gains nothing from worldly honor.

Being serious about rank and honor is distressing enough to bring tears to my eyes. Let's live with humility according to our religious principles. Paying attention to worldly honor anchors us here. We will never rise as far as heaven. Our Lord is our example. He did not lose his honor when he was humbled to death on a cross. We are going in the wrong direction when we relish temporary, earthly praise. We begin to think we have accomplished something great when we forgive someone for some small thing that was neither an insult nor a slight. We turn from this counterfeit act of forgiveness asking the Lord to "forgive us our debts as we also have forgiven our debtors" (Matt. 6:12). Help us, Lord, to perceive that we do not know what we are praying. Our hands are empty when we come to you.

—WAY

august 26

The Lord's Prayer does not say, "Forgive us because we are doing a lot of penance, frequently at prayer, fasting, and because we have entered a convent." All he teaches us to say is, "because we forgive." Christ understood that mutual love is a challenge even though it is a virtue dear to God.

Contemplatives do not pat themselves on the back. They parade their personal sins, having no desire for others to put them on a pedestal. Neither will they exhibit their family pedigree, which has no value in heaven. Being born in a good family is valuable only if it helps one serve God better. If someone is pursuing worldly honor, you may be sure that their reported progress in prayer is a devilish illusion.

—WAY

august 27
.

When I tried to resist rapture, it felt as if a great force beneath my feet lifted me up. I can think of nothing comparable—it was violently powerful. We have no power that can resist God's power. God is mightier than we are. And yes, it is startling. I remained conscious enough to know that he was lifting me up. "The hair of my flesh bristled" (Job 4:15) because I was afraid of offending God. This fear mixes with a deep love for God.

Rapture results in an odd detachment that is impossible for me to describe. It is entirely different from any other experience of prayer. It involves both the body and the spirit, releasing them from earthly constraints. An unusual pain follows rapture. I wish I could describe it. There are no words, but I will try.

I am experiencing this now. The other favors I have described came earlier, and continue to do so, but this pain is now common and frequent. The intensity varies, and one's flesh experiences it. Unless you are personally familiar with this experience, there is no way you can believe or comprehend it.

Its purpose is not consolation but a demonstration of the reason for the soul's weariness. There is a painful spiritual loneliness that royal David may have described. "I lie awake; I am like a lonely bird on the housetop" (Ps. 102:7). The extreme loneliness I feel compares with these words. It comforts me to think that someone else has experienced this. The soul is up on the roof, above all created things and living even higher than the highest part of itself.

Saint Paul said, "The world has been crucified to me, and I to the world" (Gal. 6:14). This is not true of me, I know.

But he is describing the state of an enraptured soul. There is no heavenly consolation because the soul is not in heaven. One seeks nothing from earth because it is not there either. The crucified soul hovers between heaven and earth, receiving no relief from either.

—LIFE

august 28

I read things in books on prayer that I don't fully understand. The authors advise us to discard physical images and approach contemplation of God. Thoughts of Christ's humanity hinder spiritual contemplation. They quote Jesus when he said to his disciples, "It is to your advantage that I go away, for if I do not go away, the Advocate will not come to you; but if I go, I will send him to you" (Jn. 16:7). But if they believed Jesus was both human and divine, as they did once the Holy Spirit inspired them, his physical presence would not have been a problem.

These books imply that contemplation is exclusively spiritual. They advise us to think of God as diffuse, all around us. This may be helpful once in a while, but to withdraw completely from Christ is more than I can endure. God help me to explain myself! I have no desire to contradict them, for they are educated and devout. They are guiding others. My experience is not the only way. I may be mistaken, but I will report how it happened to me.
—LIFE

august 29

In my reading, I've attempted to find parallels to my personal experiences of prayer. I once discovered a book by Bernardino de Laredo called *Ascent of the Mount*. The section that describes the union of the soul with God resonated with me. It stated that mental processes cease in this state of prayer. I marked the passage and gave the book to one of my spiritual directors. I asked him to show it to the other ecclesiastic who had been working with me. Perhaps they could decide together whether I should stop praying this way.

Spiritual directors should advise us to keep certain things secret. It's also important for them to keep secrets. I know what it's like to suffer because some of the things I have discussed with others didn't remain private. By discussing the details of my experiences with others, for good purpose, they did me much harm. They broadcast things that should have remained confidential. It appeared as though I was personally making these things public.

I gave nobleman Francisco[2] the book and told him the story of my life and sins in a general way. He shared what I said with Father Daza, and the two of them lovingly considered how to guide me. Francisco returned to me in great distress, reporting their opinion that an evil spirit was deluding me. They advised me to seek help from the Jesuits because they were highly experienced in spiritual matters. They told me my soul was in great danger, and that I should do whatever the Jesuits instruct. This disturbed me deeply and caused me to cry.

But I read in another book that God seemed to have put into my hands, "God is faithful" (1 Cor. 10:13) and would not allow Satan to deceive anyone who loves him. This gave me great consolation.

When a Jesuit came to see me, I was embarrassed and didn't want our nuns to see me conversing with such a holy servant of God, but it didn't escape their attention. The one who listened to me understood what I said. He assured me

2. Don Francisco de Salcedo, a priest the final ten years of his life, chaplain and confessor at St. Joseph.

that this was the work of God's Spirit, that I should return to my prayers, and that I still had a lot to learn. He told me I had much responsibility for what would come. He made a deep impression on me. How grand it is to understand another soul!

—LIFE

august 30
.

Oﾠne day, after lengthy prayer seeking the Lord's guidance, I began the hymn *Veni Creator*, as the Jesuit had recommended. Reciting it instantly swept me away. I heard a voice in the depth of my soul say, "I do not want you to converse with mortals, but with angels." I was frightened and comforted simultaneously.

Those words have come true. I am no longer able to form close friendships with anyone other than those who love and serve God. Small talk has become painful for me. It was as though that instant changed me into another person with enough courage to leave everything in God's hands.

—LIFE

Imagine that we have inside us a golden palace decorated with precious jewels appropriate for a great Lord. Consider that we are at least partially responsible for the beauty of this palace. No building is as attractive as a soul full of virtue. The greater the virtue the more brilliantly it shines. A great King lives in this castle. He has come from heaven to be your Father.

An idea like this will be useful in helping you recognize there is something inside you that is vastly more valuable than anything you see outside yourself. The interior of the soul is not empty. If we remember we have a Guest within us, this world's vanities could never trap us because we will know they are comparatively worthless. A hungry animal will seize whatever attracts it. We are not wild beasts.

You may laugh at my obvious comment—but listen to me. Until I turned away from the world's vanities, I didn't recognize who lived in my soul or what my soul needed. If I had known earlier that such a great King lived in the palace of my soul, I wouldn't have ignored him as I did. I would have done some housekeeping and spent time with him. How wonderful it is that one who is great enough to fill a thousand worlds agrees to confine himself to such a small place, even as he was pleased to be in Mary's womb. He has total freedom, but because of his love, he adjusts to our capacity.

—WAY

september

1

This is one of the most difficult assignments I have ever been given. I am under orders to write about prayer. I have little desire to do it. Moreover, for the past three months I have had noises in my head, and I am so dizzy it is difficult to write ordinary business letters. May God who has helped me with more difficult tasks also help me with this one.

Our soul is like a castle created from a precious jewel. There are many interesting rooms in this beautiful castle of the soul.

The soul is a paradise that God enjoys. He furnishes it with what is pure and good. The extraordinary beauty and capacity of the soul exceeds any comparison. Even the most intelligent person has no comprehension of its dimension and potential. God created it in his own likeness, which also remains beyond our mental grasp.

We don't ultimately understand ourselves or recognize who we are. Imagine not being able to tell anyone about our parents, family, and hometown. That would be less stupid than making no attempt to discover the nature of our soul. All we know is that we are living in these bodies. In faith we believe this soul exists. As for its qualities, we have little curiosity. Although the soul is the precious residence of God, we do not bother much with preserving its beauty. Our interest lies more in the setting than in the diamond and in the exterior walls of the castle—our bodies.

—CASTLE

september 2

•

Imagine a spiritual castle in our soul that contains many rooms that are beside, above, and below each other. Centered among them is the great room where secret conversation with God occurs.

Consider this image with care. God may work through what I write to reveal something about the different favors he grants to the soul. These are extremely varied, and no individual is capable of understanding all of them, especially someone as dim-witted as I. If the Lord permits you to comprehend some of this, it will be good for you to know the possibilities. If that is not one of your gifts, you can still praise God.

There is no harm in considering what waits us in heaven and of the joy experienced by the blessed. Instead, it will give us an appetite for these things. There is no risk in discovering we are able, while living in undeserving earthly exile, to love and commune with God.

—CASTLE

september 3

If you think it may be harmful for God to grant us spiritual favors here, you probably lack humility and love of neighbor. If this were not true, we would naturally be delighted that God blesses another person in this way. Moreover, what God does for someone else in no way diminishes his power to grant similar favors to us. Those who receive them are not holier than those who do not. God uses the experience of others to demonstrate his greatness and to let us praise him in his creatures.

Perhaps this idea seems unreasonable, and we should spare the weak from worrying about it. Their lack of faith does less harm than our silence. If you do not believe what I am saying, you will never discover it through your experience.

—CASTLE

september 4

.

How do we enter the castle? Is that a foolish question? After all, if the castle is your own soul you are already rather intimate with it.

What you must realize is that there are many different ways you can exist within this castle. For example, you can remain with the guards in the courtyard outside the gate. You can live your entire life and never discover what it is like inside. You may have read in a book about prayer that the soul should enter into itself. This is exactly what I'm recommending.

A knowledgeable person once compared a soul who did not pray with a paralyzed body. It has limbs and appendages but never uses them.

—CASTLE

The doorway into the castle is genuine prayer and meditation. Mechanical repetitions of prayers are insufficient. By this, I don't mean to elevate mental prayer above spoken prayer. If it is really prayer, then meditation will accompany it. If you don't consider whom you are addressing, you aren't truly praying even though you may be constantly moving your lips. If one may occasionally pray without meditating, it is only because meditation came earlier. Careless speaking to God, without reflecting upon the propriety of what you're saying, merely saying things you have memorized, is not worthy of the label "prayer." It's not appropriate for a Christian to speak to God this way. Such activity will leave you like the paralytic who waited beside the pool of Bethesda. He lay there helplessly for thirty-eight years until the Lord himself arrived to help him.

Others may enter the castle but remain preoccupied with the business of the world. They have good intentions, and sometimes they dedicate themselves to the Lord. Their casual concern for spiritual matters allows them to pray only a few times each month, distracted by thoughts of the world. "Where your treasure is, there your heart will be also" (Matt. 6:21).

—CASTLE

september 6

S ome souls who are busily involved in the affairs of the world, however shallowly, manage occasionally to enter the castle. They come into the reception rooms on the first level. Unfortunately, so many reptiles get in through the door with them that they are distracted from appreciating what the castle has to offer. But it was quite an achievement just to get inside.

If you are not such a person, you may think what I am saying is pointless. Bear with me because I can't think of any other way to explain my ideas about the interior dynamics of prayer. I'm asking the Lord to help me express concepts that may be difficult for you to understand if you have no personal experience of them. I am compelled to write of things that may not apply to all of us.

—CASTLE

•

As the creeks that flow from a crystal clear spring are as clear as the spring itself, the behavior of a gracious soul pleases both God and others. The soul is planted like a tree in the spring of life. It would produce neither shade nor fruit if it did not water its roots. The spring sustains it, preventing it from drying up, and encourages it to produce good fruit. If the soul mistakenly decides to allow itself to be transplanted beside foul water, it will become sickly and produce inferior fruit.

It is not the spring, or the bright sun at the center of the soul, that becomes cloudy. These are constantly present and nothing can mitigate their beauty. If you place a heavy cloth over a crystal sparkling in the sunshine, this barrier will prevent the sun's brilliance from affecting it.

Souls redeemed by the blood of Jesus Christ, understand yourselves and have mercy on yourselves! If you perceive your nature, you will naturally want to cleanse yourself of anything that darkens you. O Jesus! It saddens me to see a soul deprived of your light. The rooms of this castle are unkempt because the housekeepers, our senses and faculties, ignore the need.

—CASTLE

september 8

I know someone who received two special favors from God. The first was an elevated concern about being offensive to God. She continually begged God to help her avoid that. The second was a humbling mirror in which she could not see any of her good deeds as her own product, but rather the result of God's love and warmth flowing through her. She reports that this became so vivid that whenever she did anything good or observed a good act, she immediately understood God was the source of it. Rather than consider herself as having anything to do with it, she praised God.

You will not waste your reading time (or my time writing) if these two blessings become yours.

—Castle

B e patient with me. It is not easy to explain things about the interior life. We hear that prayer is valuable and we are urged to pray. There is good advice on how to pray, but very little is said about the supernatural work of the Lord in a soul. It should be helpful, then, for me to describe and explain this heavenly castle inside us.

I have already mentioned that our spiritual castle has many rooms. Don't think of these rooms as neatly aligned down a hallway. Think of concentric spheres with the palace of the King at the center. Many rooms surround that central core in all directions, layer upon layer. It is impossible to exaggerate the potential of the soul. The Sun at the center illumines all of it. The praying soul must be free to explore this great variety of rooms. It should not hide in a corner but frequently linger in the room of humbling self-knowledge, considering the greatness and majesty of God.

Regardless of the refinement your soul may have attained, self-knowledge remains important. Humility must keep working like a bee making honey. This is essential. Notice how the bee constantly flies around from one flower to another.

Sometimes the soul will emerge from self-knowledge like a bee from its hive and fly up while meditating upon the greatness and majesty of God. This is better than thinking about its own nature, and it becomes free of the reptiles that infest these first rooms of self-knowledge. We reach much greater heights by considering the virtue of God than by confining ourselves to our own little space.

—CASTLE

september 10

Knowledge of yourself is critically important. Even if you were lifted up into heaven, I would not want you to ease your search for personal understanding.

Humility is our chief concern as long as we remain on earth. It is best for us to enter the room where we gain humility rather than to go flying off into the other rooms. This is the road that takes us where we want to go. There is no point in wishing we had wings when we have a safe, smooth road to travel.

We will never know ourselves unless we attempt to know God. Consider the greatness of God and then return to our own smallness. Look toward God's purity and you will discover your filthiness. Meditate upon God's humility and you will perceive your own lack of humility.

—CASTLE

september 11

•

Instead of thinking in terms of a few rooms in this spiritual castle, think of a million rooms. Souls have many different ways of being here. The devil, though, has planted many temptations in all these places to mislead souls attempting to pass from one room to another. A thousand tricks trap a naive soul. This doesn't work as well on those who are nearer where the King resides, but these outer rooms are still full of worldly things. We don't have the strength at this point to become free of pleasure and egotism, honors and affectations. We are quickly defeated, even while we intend to do good and live decently.

Under these circumstances, it is important that we frequently turn to God, seeking divine assistance.

—CASTLE

september 12

Contrast is revealing. Something white seems whiter beside something black, and blackness looks darker next to whiteness. If we turn our attention away from ourselves and toward God, our thoughts will become nobler and quicker to accept superior ideas. If we never rise above our personal issues, we deny ourselves an advantage.

If we remain dominated by our human nature we will never break free of cowardice and fear. Self-consciously we will ask, "Are others watching me? Are there hazards along this path? Is this something I dare begin to do? Does pride motivate my desire? Am I too sinful to pray? Will people respect me for my independence? Aren't extremes a bad thing even regarding virtue? Suppose I fail?"

God knows how many souls the devil has ruined with such questions. They imagine their misgivings spring from humility, but they are the result of a lack of self-knowledge. Our human nature overwhelms us. We need to look at Christ, who will teach us humility.

—Castle

september 13

There are many first rooms of prayer in the interior castle. The soul enters them by various means.

Many temptations and distractions await us here. All kinds of devilish deceptions hinder us from wandering among this multiplicity of rooms. The nearer we advance toward the King's dwelling area, the less effective these become, but in these outer rooms the soul remains preoccupied with worldly business and pleasure.

We may wish to honor God and do good works, but our ambition and senses work against us. When we experience this tension, we should turn toward our merciful God for help.

—CASTLE

september 14

Light emanating from the King's palace is quite dim near the entrance. Darkness here is not complete, but it is enough to conceal things about ourselves.

I'm finding it difficult to express this idea. Snakes and other poisonous creatures that enter right along with us can fill these spaces. Such things interfere with our perception of the light. It is as though we were in a brightly lit place but have dust and grit in our squinting eyes. We close our eyes and perceive nothing but ourselves. Such a soul is not in a harmful state, but it remains blind to the castle's beauty.

To proceed deeper into the interior castle you will need to discard any unnecessary possessions, honors, and business. This is an important step. Unless we take it, we will hamper our spiritual progress.

—CASTLE

september 15

What is it like to have broken free of earthly encumbrances, penetrated more deeply into various rooms of the castle, and then return to the hubbub of life? We can easily fall prey to a setback. Few of the rooms in this castle are off limits to devils. Our faculties are strong enough to combat them, but we must never fail to be on guard. "Even Satan disguises himself as an angel of light"

(2 Cor. 11:14). He has many methods that gradually hurt us. We usually don't recognize what is happening until after the injury.

Here is an example of what I mean: a person may begin to practice penance, but if this good desire becomes a force of disobedience it can be harmful. When penitential activity continues even after it ceases to be good for you, it may become harmful.

—CASTLE

september 16

We discover true perfection in love of God and neighbor. The better we keep these two commandments, the more perfect we will be. The rule we follow helps us keep our Lord's instructions.

Mutual love is of primary importance.

A soul can destroy its own peace and disturb the peace of others by allowing trifling things to distract it. When we are ignorant and don't have all the facts before us, we can mistakenly see imperfection where it does not exist.

—CASTLE

september 17

Those who already know how to pray can begin to hear the Lord's voice. We remain busy with our jobs and recreation, we continue to give in to temptations, but the Lord is able to get through to us. The attractive things we hear create a tension in us that we wouldn't feel in the castle rooms where the noises of the world drown out his voice.

We don't hear the voice of the Lord the way it will be heard when we've penetrated into the castle more deeply. Now he speaks to us through other people. Perhaps we hear a sermon or read a book. God has many ways of speaking to us. Perhaps we are sick or in trouble, or we pray a brief prayer. His Majesty patiently waits for many days, years.

Meanwhile the devil makes more vicious attacks on the soul. O my Lord! Your assistance is necessary here. Have mercy and prevent this soul from being led astray right at the beginning. Give it enough light to find its way into this good castle.

—CASTLE

september 18

Don't expect anything special, spiritually, at the beginning. Your objective is to lay a foundation. It will rain manna later, when you are in the interior rooms.

Smile with me! We are still beginners, encumbered with thousands of faults and blemishes, or virtues barely able to walk on frail, new legs, and we are looking for favors! His Majesty knows what is best for us. It is not our business to tell him what to give us.

The beginner has only one assignment: work hard at making your will conform to God's will. This is important. Don't forget it.

—CASTLE

september 19

Is there anything worse than being uncomfortable in your own home? There's no chance that we will ever find rest outside of ourselves if we are not resting within. We have no choice but to live with our physical faculties. They are our relatives and friendly visitors. We may wish we were alone, but we are required to entertain them. Our vices have distorted our view of them, making them seem to be at war with us.

"Peace. Be still!" Our Lord frequently spoke this command. Trust me, if we can't discover peace in our own home, we will never realize it outside. Stop fighting. Through the blood Christ shed for us I say to anyone who has not yet turned inward, do it now. If you have already started to do this, don't let the conflict turn you away. A relapse can be worse than the original illness. Trust God's mercy rather than yourself. His Majesty will lift you from one level to another until you are beyond the reach of wild things and blessings abound. We don't accomplish this by force, but by gentleness.

If you stumble, don't give up. God will even work something good out of your fall. The only cure for neglecting to pray is to start praying again.

—Castle

B ecause I told you that turning back is so bad, you might get the idea that it is better to remain outside this castle. "If you live dangerously, it will kill you" (Sir. 3:26 TEV). We are foolish if we think we will ever enter heaven without first entering into ourselves, knowing ourselves, recognizing our misery, realizing how much we owe God, and begging for his mercy. Our Lord says, "No one comes to the Father except through me" (Jn. 14:6). I haven't looked it up, but I think he also says, "Whoever has seen me has seen the Father" (Jn. 14:9). If we never see him or think about how much we owe him because of the death he suffered on our behalf, there is no way we will be able to know and serve him. What is the value of faith without works? What good are our works if they are not connected with the merits of Jesus Christ?

May it please His Majesty to let us see how much we cost him and that "a disciple is not above the teacher, nor a slave above the master" (Matt. 10:24). We are required to make an effort if we intend to enjoy God's glory. We need to pray for this insight; otherwise, we may enter into temptation.

—CASTLE

september 21

Happy are those who fear the Lord, who greatly delight in his commandments" (Ps. 112:1). If we don't turn back now, we are certainly on the way to salvation.

We are miserable living under siege, with weapons under the table and beside the bed, always waiting for a surprise attack. It is a blessing to be secure among the blessed.

O my Lord, do you want us to have a miserable life? We desire to stop asking you to deliver us from it, unless we may lose it for you or consume it in your service. We wish we could understand what you want for us. If it is your will, we will die for you. As St. Thomas said, living without you and the fear of losing you are nothing other than dying.

If our happiness is pleasing God, then we will never be happy with such worries. Remember there were some extraordinary saints who succumbed to serious temptations.

—CASTLE

september 22

W riting this disturbs me. I know you want me to live a holy life. I want that too, but I am not doing very well at it. Here I am writing something for people who could teach me! I am following orders, but this is not an easy command to obey. Because I am doing this for God, I pray that God will use my work to be of some value for you. God knows the only thing I can boast about is his mercy.

Let me return to an idea I was trying to express about souls dwelling in this castle. The Lord has favored them greatly by bringing them through beginners' struggles. Many such persons have reached higher rooms. They don't want to offend God, and they regularly do penance, are charitable toward others, guard their speech and manner of dress, and take care of business. This is an excellent condition for anyone. I can see no reason why they should not progress to the final dwelling places.

—CASTLE

september 23

After having come this far, we want to press on to the highest good. But we need more before we can live completely in Christ. It is not enough simply to desire it, the way the young man asked Jesus, "What good deed must I do to have eternal life?" (Matt. 19:16). This young man has been on my mind since I began to write about these rooms. He is an exact parallel to our condition. It is good to make this inquiry, but it's only a beginning. Move on from here, but accept the fact that you are God's servant. If you desire too much, you may lose what you have. Consider the saints who previously entered this chamber and you will recognize the difference between them and us.

If we behave like the young man in the Gospel and sadly turn away after the Lord tells us what he requires of us, what do you then want God to do? What God gives is in relation to our love for him. This love is not something we can imagine, but we demonstrate it by the way we live.

—CASTLE

Our work is not finished when we abandon our possessions the way St. Peter walked away from his fishing nets. Renunciation of this kind is only a preparation. We still need to be careful to stay away from the vermin that are present in the outer rooms of this castle. Have the desire to progress deeper. If you persevere, you will reach your goal.

Listen to me and understand that your perseverance includes considering yourself a "worthless slave" (Lk. 17:10) who has no right to expect favors from our Lord. The more you receive, the more you are indebted. I'm not able to think of other ways to explain this, but the Lord will help you to understand. He will help you gain humility out of spiritual dryness rather than the uneasiness that comes without him. When you are humble God gives peace and contentment. We have more affection for God's consolations than for the cross. Examine us, Lord. You know the truth. Help us to know ourselves.

—CASTLE

september 25

M any souls reach the upper dwelling places of the interior castle and reside in them for years with orderly lives. They become falsely confident and comfortable. When His Majesty prods them with a small disturbance they become unreasonably distressed. They will not listen to advice. They thought they could teach others when suddenly they sink into despair.

Nothing I've ever tried is any help for their misery. All I can do is feel compassion for them. Because they think they are experiencing spiritual difficulties for God, they are not able to perceive their disturbance as an imperfection. It could be that noticing their fault is more troubling than whatever triggers it. God's mercy is in their discomfort because it prompts humility.

If we test ourselves before God tests us, we will be prepared when God's testing comes.

—Castle

Suppose someone who is rich and without heirs suddenly loses a lot of money. Sufficient funds remain for daily living plus a little surplus to save. Now if this individual reacts as though *everything* is lost, how can the Lord ask for additional sacrifice?

If another chance to earn a handsome income arrives, the individual should accept it. But striving for more and more, even with good intentions such as helping the poor, is not likely to be compatible with drawing nearer the inner dwelling places.

The same thing happens when others reject or dishonor us. Life's difficulties are a favor from God, but usually they disturb us. Amazing! We have long considered how the Lord suffered and how we may suffer with him. The salve for our wounds is humility. After a while, the Lord will come to heal us.

—CASTLE

september 27
.

At this stage there is a strong desire for penance. There is nothing wrong with this, as long as there is no damage done to your health. But it isn't satisfactory to spend too much time here. We have a long way yet to go.

Serving God one step at a time means we will never finish our journey.

Because this traveling wearies us, we will likely stray off the path. Don't tarry. If we could go from one place to another in eight days, why take a year to do it? The rough road will expose us to bad weather and threats of all kinds. It will be better to make the trip quickly.

—Castle

september 28
.

We don't have the option of letting others walk this path for us. We will have to make the effort ourselves. Let's leave our reason and fears in our Lord's hands.

Anything less is nothing but distraction. Care about nothing other than drawing closer to the Lord. You may have little or no reassurance now, but there is nothing to worry about. Similarly, fretting about your health will not improve your health. I have discovered this for myself. And this is spiritual business that does not involve our bodies.

This journey requires humility, and a lack of it will detain us for a lifetime. We will be burdened with a load of earthly nature, most of which has been set aside by those who penetrate more deeply into the castle. Comparing yourself with them, you will think you have made only a few steps of progress.

—CASTLE

september 29
•

Without humility, we will linger here the rest of our lives and be afflicted with a thousand miseries. If we haven't discarded preoccupation with ourselves, we will find exploration of this castle both difficult and tedious. We'll be traveling with a cumbersome burden of human nature that those who ascend higher have shed. But even at this elementary level, our just and merciful Lord gives us blessings. We may depend upon him to give us much more than we deserve, and his consolations are superior to any we may find in the pleasures of the physical life. God's reason for giving us a small taste of spiritual delight at this point in our development may be to encourage us to prepare for more.

—CASTLE

september 30

I can tell you there was a time when I didn't know anything about consolations and spiritual delights. I certainly didn't expect to experience them. I was content to think my behavior was pleasing God. I read about the delights and favors God grants to those who serve him, and I praised him for it. But if one person who reads this is prompted to praise God, I think it is a good thing the subject came up.

Everyone should have someone to consult about religious matters. We get into trouble when we follow our own desires. The achievements of others can inspire us. What seems impossible for us may appear easy when we see them do it. When fledglings learn to fly, they do not immediately soar but follow parental guidance a little at a time.

—CASTLE

october

I need to repeat my request to the Holy Spirit that I will be inspired to say something helpful to you. Now I begin to write of the supernatural.

The next group of beautiful rooms in the interior castle is nearer to the King's palace. You may think you will have to be in the other rooms a long time before you can enter here. But there is no rigid requirement. The Lord's blessings are his to give when, as, and to whom he wills. Since no one has any right to any of them, no one is ever slighted.

It is rare to encounter any poisonous creatures in these rooms. The few that are here are harmless, perhaps even beneficial.

—CASTLE

october 2

L et me describe the difference between consolations and joy in prayer. Consolations are experiences that result from our meditation and requests. Although God is certainly involved in the process, joy and peace begin with our own effort.

Remember that Jesus said, "Apart from me you can do nothing" (Jn. 15:5)—but we should still recognize our behavior as a contributor to our prayerful consolations. This doesn't mean you've earned them. You can probably remember similar feelings in other experiences. You may inherit a lot of money, or suddenly see someone you love, or have success in a huge business venture, or see a husband, brother, or son after you understood he was dead. These great consolations will cause tears to flow. Simply expressed, when we pray, joyful consolations start in our human nature and end in God.

O Jesus, I wish I could explain this! I don't know how to describe the difference I see. There is a verse in the Psalm that ends, "you enlarge my understanding" (Ps. 119:32). These words affirm the difference for anyone who has experienced it, but anyone else needs me to say more about it.

—CASTLE

october 3

The consolations I've mentioned do not develop the heart. If I knew more about the nature of human mentality I might be able to explain this more clearly. My knowledge of sensuality and human nature is limited. My personal experience is not enough to permit me to express these things in words.

I will try to describe my experience of the consolation and joy produced by meditation. I wish I could explain the difference between consolation and joy. I'm not ready yet to say which one I think is better, but I do want to point out the distinctive quality of each.

If I began to shed tears when I considered Christ's passion, I wouldn't stop until I got a horrible headache. If the subject were my personal sins, the same thing would happen. Our Lord did me this favor. An individual's temperament may encourage such tears, but they ultimately end in God. If you have the humility to comprehend that you aren't superior to others because you shed them, you may value them highly. If they are the result of love, they are God's gift to you.

—CASTLE

october 4

•

L ove is more important than thought. Do what inspires you to love.

Our concept of love may be shallow. Great pleasure is not its chief feature. Instead, love brings a strong desire to please God and causes us to be careful not to offend God. Love makes us want to see an increase in the honor and glory of God's Son and the advancement of his church. If you are distracted a little now and then, that does not mean you have stopped loving.

I have also struggled with this problem. About four years ago I noticed that an imaginative mind is not equal to intelligence. Intelligence is one of the soul's functions, and it worried me that mine could sometimes become restless. The human mind is a busy thing and only God can hold it still. It has seemed to me that my soul could be absorbed in God while my mind was distracted.

As we cannot stop the movement of the stars in the sky, neither can we control our mind. When we are distracted as we pray, it does not mean we are wasting time with God. The soul may be wrapped up in God at the center of the castle while the mind remains outside skirmishing with many wild and poisonous creatures. We should not let this disturbance discourage us from prayer.

—CASTLE

october 5

•

As I write this, my head is roaring with noise. It's as though rivers rushing through rapids filled my head. Birds whistle and chirp from the trees. This noise does not come through my ears but originates in my cranium.

Perhaps the Lord gave me this headache to help me understand these spiritual things. This cacophony in my head does not get in the way of prayer or writing. Actually, my soul is absolutely quiet. Although these miseries seem to be taunting the soul, the Lord frees us from them in the ultimate dwelling place. Don't blame the soul for what a poor imagination, human nature, and the devil may be causing.

—CASTLE

october 6

.

I want to describe what I call the Prayer of Quiet. Anyone who has experienced this should understand what I mean.

Think of it this way: Two ponds of water have quite different sources. One needs elaborate plumbing with canals and pipes. An unseen, continuously flowing spring fills the other. The pipes are like our meditations that bring us the water when we have done our work. But the spring is symbolic of a direct gift from God. I can't say where or how it arrives. All I can say is that it begins with God and ends within ourselves, producing a great calm and peace.

God enlarges the heart by sending spiritual water from a source deep within us. It is like smelling something cooking on a distant grill. The spiritual joy is not something we can obtain with our own efforts. We can only receive it as a gift. The best way to experience it, then, is not to strive for it. Simply love God without any ulterior motives. In humility, recognize that you are not worthy of such an experience. Instead of seeking spiritual pleasure, desire to suffer the way the Lord suffered.

God knows what is best for us. Is there any way that we can make a spring flow water? There is nothing we can do.

This experience is given only as God wills, and often we are not even thinking about it.
—CASTLE

october 7

·

For me, water is the best comparison for spiritual experiences. I'm not very clever, but I have carefully observed the nature of water.

I believe there are helpful secrets in everything our great and wise God has created, and if we will notice them we will benefit from them. There's more than we can comprehend in the smallest things created by God. We can learn from the little ant.

When our heart expands as the psalmist mentions, this doesn't originate in the heart itself. It comes from somewhere deeper, more interior, from the center of the soul. We have secrets within us that often astonish me, and there must be many more I have never observed.

O my Lord and my God, how majestic are your wonders! We wander around foolishly down here, believing that we are gaining some knowledge of you. The fragment we grasp is next to nothing. We don't even understand ourselves.

—CASTLE

october 8

·

Once spiritual water begins to flow from this spring in the depths of our soul, it expands our interior being. We do not understand the resulting blessings. We catch the scent of it, as though from a distant grill. We don't perceive the glow of the coals, but we feel the warmth and sense the fragrant aromas.

Don't misunderstand me. These are not physical sensations. They are subliminal, ineffable. I am attempting to explain this using a metaphor to help you comprehend. The experience is far more delicate and subtle than you might expect. Nonetheless, it is an actual experience that the soul understands more clearly than I have described. It is beyond anything you might imagine, consisting of material far more precious than our commonplace human components.

—CASTLE

•

The true value of prayer is that it unites our will with God's will. This results in the sort of life we live following prayer. These effects are the best test of authentic prayer.

Even though there is much about it we will never understand, God's drawing the soul nearer to himself is something desirable.

There are times when the Lord grants such a moment simply because he wants to do so. God knows why and we don't need to concern ourselves with the reason for it. By now you have accomplished some necessary preparation. Humility is the key. By humility the Lord opens himself to us. The best indicator that you have humility is that you feel unworthy of the favors our Lord grants you and you would not expect to experience them in this life.

—CASTLE

october 10

I want to mention a kind of prayer that is a precursor to all of the above. It is a supernatural recollection that is not dependent upon closed eyes or darkness. Nothing outside us enters the equation. Eye closure is involuntary and the soul wants to be alone. We contribute nothing to the construction of a temple, a place where the soul may enter to pray. External things diminish, as the soul grows stronger.

Others have described this prayer as the soul entering itself or rising above itself. This language is of no help. I have another way of presenting it that may be easier for you to understand, but I admit I may be the only one who understands what I am attempting to explain.

Some residents of this interior castle have been wandering outside its wall for years. Now and then they take a few steps toward the door. When the great King sees their good intentions, he mercifully wants to call them in. Like a good shepherd, he makes a call so gentle as to be almost inaudible. But it is enough. They recognize his voice and return. The call of the Shepherd has a powerful effect. They drop external diversions and come.

I think that's the best I've ever explained it! I don't know how they hear. It isn't with their ears because there is no sound. But there is a perception of gentle shrinking inside. I have read that it's like a hedgehog or a turtle drawing into itself. The important difference is that it is not done voluntarily, but only when His Majesty grants the favor.

—CASTLE

october 11

The prayer of recollection I have described prepares us for listening. The soul, rather than working to converse with God, remains passive and notices that the Lord is at work.

The advice of others that we should turn off our minds is a futile suggestion. We can't do it. In prayer the less we think and the less we do, the greater the results. Our task is to be a beggar at a rich person's door, and then lower our gaze and humbly wait.

When we perceive he has heard us it is time to fall silent. If we are not sure anyone has noticed us, there is no merit in acting foolishly. We become fools if we attempt to make this prayer happen. Spiritual dryness results and our imaginations become active.

Our Lord wants us to call for him and recognize that we are in his presence. He knows what's best for us. Let's leave that to him. Such moments of prayer are peaceful and quiet. Making a strenuous effort is out of place and is not productive. Trust your soul to God's care, allowing him to do what he wills with it. Submit yourself to the will of God. The most pleasing thing to God is for us to forget ourselves and concentrate on his honor and glory.

—CASTLE

october 12

•

When God is ready for us to limit our thoughts, he occupies our minds with a light that is far above anything we can produce on our own. We become absorbed in this light and we receive superior instruction. Make no effort to understand this spiritual recollection in God. Let the soul effortlessly enjoy it, responding with nothing more than a few words of love.

I am describing the kind of prayer that flows from a spring rather than through pipes and trenches. This prayer is less intense than a prayer of spiritual delight. It's an introduction, a beginning, an expanding of the soul. It's like a fountain that doesn't release its water into a stream. Instead, it enlarges its trough as it accepts more water.

Such an experience of prayer will increase faith and improve all one's virtues. Then every spiritual discipline becomes possible.

—CASTLE

october 13

•

Let me warn you about a danger. Some persons have such weak physical constitutions that any interior pleasure quickly overcomes them. They misinterpret what is happening to them and call the physical experience "spiritual." They figure it must be rapture. I call it foolishness.[3] But it's a waste of time and bad for their health.

3. A typical Teresan pun: *arrobamiento*, rapture; *abobamiento*, foolishness.

When God gives you a spiritual experience there is no withering weakness in the soul, only deep joy at being close to God. It lasts but for a moment of time and there is no external sensation.

Always praise God. Amen.

—CASTLE

october 14

•

Most people are able to enter the upper rooms of the castle, but some do so more consistently than others. "Many are called, but few are chosen" (Matt. 22:14). The experience here is that of an unquestionable union of the soul with God.

Regarding the soul's union with God, there is no more certain proof that this has happened than our personal abandonment. This union is not similar to a dream. It may seem that the soul is asleep, but it isn't. In this state, it is not necessary to practice any special technique to push back activity of the mind. We are already completely disassociated from physical things. As long as the union continues, the soul is unaware of sensory perception. Thinking is not possible. At this level, we have died to the world in order to live in God.

—CASTLE

october 15

•

I wish I could explain God's secrets. If it would help anyone, I would utter a thousand foolish comments. Perhaps a few of them will make sense and result in great praise to God.

Perhaps I have disturbed you by saying "*if* the prayer is union with God," suggesting there are other unions possible. This is a genuine possibility. If we love other things, the devil will use them to carry us away. But it's not the same thing. Such a moment doesn't come with the same satisfaction, peace, and joy. Union with God is far above any earthly pleasure. It is distinctively different, as rough skin is different from bone marrow. That's it. I don't know any way to express it more succinctly.

—CASTLE

october 16

·

You and I still want clearer understanding. Interior things are not easy to explain. My comments up to this point are satisfactory for someone who has experienced union with God, but I need to give clearer indications to eliminate any concerns regarding the authenticity of the experience. I admit that I am expressing personal opinion. I remain willing to listen to those who are more educated than I am. God has prepared others to guide the church. They are able to evaluate the thoughts others express. If they don't already know the answer to a question, they know how to look for it in their books.

The soul's union with God is brief and perceived as shorter than it probably is. The experience is unforgettable. Years may pass, but the soul will never doubt the authenticity of the event. It was in God and God was in it. I honestly don't know how this works, but I know I'm telling the truth. If this certainty is missing, I doubt that union of the soul with God ever occurred.

—Castle

The bride says, "He brought me to the banqueting house, and his intention toward me was love" (S. of S. 2:4). She does not say she went, but rather "he *brought* me." This banqueting house, or wine cellar, is where the Lord takes us when he desires. We are with him there on his terms, not ours. We aren't able to enter on our terms regardless of our effort. His Majesty must take us into the center of our soul. Because he wants to demonstrate his wonder as clearly as possible, he doesn't want us to have any part to play. We must totally surrender to him. The door of our wits and senses remains closed. He enters the soul's center without going through any door, the same way he entered the room where his disciples were when he said, "Peace be with you" (Jn. 20:19).

Eventually, we will see how His Majesty wants the soul to enjoy him in the center of itself even more than here. We will see so much if we understand we are unworthy servants of a Lord who is beyond our comprehension. May he be forever praised.

You may think I have already said all there is to say about these dwelling places. That is not the case, because one's experience at each level comes in varying degrees of intensity. There's not much more I can say about the nature of union with God, but there is a lot remaining regarding the Lord's activity in a prepared soul.

—CASTLE

october 18

.

Let me illustrate what happens to the soul by comparing it with an example from nature. When spring brings new leaves to mulberry trees, silkworms hatch from tiny eggs. The worms feed on the leaves until they mature. They then spin silk and hide themselves in cocoons. The ugly worm dies and a lovely white moth emerges from the cocoon. This is an astonishing, unbelievable event! If we heard it in a story, we wouldn't believe it.

The experiences of the silkworm and the soul are similar. The soul starts to live when warmed by the Holy Spirit and feeds upon the nourishments provided by the church.

When it is mature it spins its silk and begins to build the house in which to die, the house of Christ. I can't quote the verse exactly, but I have heard that our lives are hidden with Christ in God and that real life is Christ. [See Col. 3:3-4.]

In the prayer of union, God himself becomes our house. We can weave a little cocoon by eliminating selfishness and any attachment to earthly things and by practicing the teachings of the church. Let this silkworm die. Let it die. Dying is what it was born to do. Death fulfills its purpose.

And here is my point: when the silkworm dies to the world, out comes a little white moth. Oh, the greatness of God! Imagine! A soul in this prayer is enclosed in God's greatness for a little while—I think not much more than half an hour—and it is transformed. It no longer recognizes itself. There is now all the difference between an ugly worm and a little white moth. The soul understands it has done nothing to deserve this blessing. All it wants to do now is to praise the Lord. It is willing to die a thousand deaths for him.

—CASTLE

october 19

•

Now see the restlessness of this little moth in spite of the fact that it has never been more relaxed in its life. Its problem is that it doesn't know where to land. Every place it sees on earth is unsatisfactory. The food that pleased the worm won't do for the moth. Weaving a cocoon is of no interest when you have wings. Where will it go? It can't return to its beginnings. Although at peace, the soul will feel an inescapable pain because of this. The only possible solace comes from the realization that God desires it to live in this exile.

As the moth lays new eggs, produces additional silkworms, and then dies, so God wants others to benefit from the favors he gives us. It is important, then, to love our neighbors with God's love.

—Castle

october 20

Even though I have written at length, there is more I could say. If you've experienced divine favors, you know that I have not reported everything.

It is not surprising that this little butterfly doesn't feel at home in this world. Where will it find rest? It's not able to return by its own desire and effort to the condition

God freely grants. New struggles follow such a transcendent favor.

This doesn't mean that we have no peace after such moments. We do, and it's a deeply gratifying peace. Even our spiritual stress produces peace and joy. The understanding that God *wants* us to live in this alien world brings relief by itself. But our difficulty springs from the fact that we are not yet completely surrendered to God.

—Castle

october 21

·

The heartache we feel in worldly experience does not penetrate the deepest places of our being the way that spiritual pain can. The soul breaks into fragments without any desire or effort on its part. I want to explain this.

God brought the bride into the deepest wine cellar, "and his intention toward me was love" (S. of S. 2:4). This is how it is. The soul completely surrenders itself into God's hands. God is its only interest. God impresses his seal upon the soul, and it has no more involvement in the process than warm wax.

—Castle

october 22

•

We may describe our soul as a little butterfly or a dove. Having received a favor from God, it must continue in God's service. It is not as though it has already arrived at a destination.

This is not the time to become careless and stray from the heavenly path. If we fail to keep God's commandments we will suffer the same fate as the silkworm. It releases its seed to produce more silkworms and then dies.

God will not allow such a great favor without good results. If we do not receive benefit from it, others will. The soul retains enough desire and virtue to affect other souls in the same way that the flame of a torch will ignite another torch. Even if the fire goes out, a desire to help others will linger.

I know someone who went far astray but continued to enjoy guiding others regarding the nature of prayer. She did a lot of good by helping them to understand, and then later, the Lord gave her light.

—CASTLE

october 23

·

In spite of everything I've said about this place where we dwell with God, I still have not made it clear. I don't want to give the impression that you are without hope if the Lord doesn't give you this spiritual gift. You may yet experience genuine union with God if you focus your attention exclusively upon seeking God's will. Many of us say we don't want anything else and are willing to die if it is God's will.

Let me repeat: if what you say is true, you have received this favor from the Lord and you don't need to desire anything beyond it. There is happiness in this for any soul. A soul in this condition will be tranquil here as well as in heaven. Nothing on earth will disturb it because it will trust the Lord's wisdom. Suffering will continue, but it will also pass without disturbing the deepest places.

—CASTLE

october 24

·

Union with God's will is the union I have sought.

Sadly, few of us experience this kind of union. When we think we are being careful not to offend the Lord and enter a religious life, we sometimes think we've done everything possible. As a result, our experience parallels that of Jonah who "made a booth for himself there. He sat under it in the shade, waiting to see what would become of the city. The Lord God appointed a bush, and made it come up over Jonah, to give shade over his head, to save him from his discomfort. . . . But when dawn came up the next day, God appointed a worm that attacked the bush, so that it withered" (Jonah 4:5–7). Such worms can chew away our virtues. This is the result of self-love, passing judgment on others, and issues such as not loving our neighbors as ourselves. We may continue to crawl, fulfilling our obligation and not committing any sin, but we never get near complete union with the will of God.

—Castle

october 25

Can you define God's will? God wants us perfectly united with him. Putting that on paper brings me much pain because I am so far away from this union. He asks for only two things, that we love him and love our neighbor. If we do this we are on the road to spiritual perfection.

The best way to determine whether or not we are keeping both of these laws is to notice how well we love our neighbor. It is nearly impossible to know if we truly love God, but we may certainly perceive our love of neighbor. These two loves progress in harmony. The more we love our neighbor, the more we will love God. Give careful attention to this. We will never have a perfect love for our neighbor unless we have based it on love of God.

—Castle

october 26

Some people are grimly serious about prayer. They rigidly control their thoughts to confine every scrap of devotion. They don't understand how we receive union with God.

They think they must be gloomy about it. This is absolutely wrong. The Lord is watching our behavior among others. He wants to see you help someone who is sick. He wants you to be sympathetic and caring. If someone else receives praise, God wants you to be happier than if someone had praised you. If you notice a fault in another person, hide it as though it belonged to you.

If we fail to love our neighbor there is no hope for us. Beg the Lord to perfect your love of neighbor. Turn God loose with this. He will give you more than you can seek.

—CASTLE

october 27

How may you receive God's graces without seeking them? Don't look for them. It is primarily important to love God without any self-interest. To think that we can earn something so great with our miserable services indicates a lack of humility. Our preparation for these divine favors is to desire to suffer the way our Lord suffered rather than to enjoy spiritual pleasure.

God is under no obligation to grant favors to us. Many good Christians never experience them. God knows what's best for us, and he knows who truly loves him. I am certain of this. Therefore, all our efforts would be in vain. You cannot draw this water through pipes, and we will tire of digging at a spring. Regardless of the time we spend meditating and tearfully trying to wring something out, this water will not flow. It comes only to those God wants to have it, and often when the soul least expects it.

—CASTLE

october 28

·

You are familiar with the concept of the soul becoming God's spiritual spouse. Bless God that in his mercy he desires to be humbled. The comparison may be crude, but I can think of no better parallel relationship than marriage. Love unites with love in a pure and delicate way.

The prayer of union does not become spiritual betrothal right away. In human society, when two people become engaged we discuss their relationship. Do they love each other? Are they becoming more acquainted with each other?

Have they stopped seeking someone else? In the same way, we make an agreement in this union with God. The soul is familiar with its spouse and committed to faithfulness. His Majesty clearly perceives this and shows great mercy as they meet together.

—CASTLE

october 29

•

I tell you, I have known people who have come this high with God and attained this union who were turned back by the devil's craftiness and deception. All the powers of hell work furiously to block the progress of one soul, because that soul can influence so many others for good.

Martyrs have converted thousands. The young girl St. Ursula and founders of religious orders such as St. Dominic and St. Francis have helped us so much because they received favors from God. This would never have happened if they hadn't carefully held on to their spiritual gain.

God needs us now more than ever, because there are not many today who care about honoring him. God, enlighten us. Don't let us fall into darkness.

—CASTLE

october 30

•

If the soul is committed to the will of God, how can it be deceived? If it wants nothing other than to do God's will, why would it turn aside? We could understand that if we were still committed to the world, but at this point God has granted us such great mercy it would seem impossible. Still, remember how Judas was Christ's companion and heard him when he spoke. There is no security in this. The devil arrives with skillful deception, confusing us by making evil look good. He gradually darkens our intellect and cools our devotion.

How does the devil do it? What are his tricks? There is no private place where he cannot enter, no desert remote enough that he fails to travel there. The Lord may permit this in order to watch the behavior of a soul for which he has great designs. If there is going to be a defeat, it is better that it happen here at the beginning instead of later when it could harm so many.

—CASTLE

october 31

Our most effective defense against the devil's attacks is prayer. We ask God to sustain us, knowing that if we are abandoned we will quickly fall into a spiritual abyss. We must not trust our own strength. Then we need to pay special attention to practicing virtue in our daily lives. Are our love for others and our humility growing? God will help us to see these things.

You have come a long way. You are now intimate with God. Having reached this boundary, you must not fall asleep.

—CASTLE

november

1
•

Now, with the assistance of the Holy Spirit, I will tell of the rooms in the castle where the soul wants to be alone with its Spouse.

Some people will accuse you of being holier-than-thou, a self-righteous show-off. Friends will desert you. They will say the devil has led you astray and they will even laugh at you. And if they should praise you, that will be a trial also. Eventually the soul will disregard the praise and find the criticism a joy.

Illness may also become a problem. I know a person who hasn't been without pain since God granted her this favor forty years ago. There have been other difficulties as well. It seems to me that the Lord allows the devil to try the soul to the point that it thinks God has rejected it.

Suffering like this will enable the soul to enter these rooms. Such hazards only make the moth fly higher.

—CASTLE

november 2

We may experience difficulty because of an inexperienced confessor who is uncertain and cautious about experiences he thinks are unusual. He will assume that anyone who could report such results of meditation must be an angel. If he then perceives some imperfection in you, he will doubt the authenticity of your experience. He will condemn it as an evil gift from the devil or the product of your own sadness. And why not? The devil is extraordinarily active, and sadness is commonplace in the world today.

Any condemnation of our spiritual experience causes us great grief. You will need to go through this distress to understand what I mean. Self-doubt easily follows. We will think God has allowed us to be deceived because we have lived a wretched life. The spiritual favor lasts but for a moment; we remember our sins always. We have no difficulty finding our own faults. When the confessor raises his doubts, our anguish intensifies. We will believe we have never been with God and never will be. When we hear someone speak of God, it is as though we are hearing about someone far away.

Making matters worse is the realization that we cannot find any words that will explain our experiences adequately. It seems that God allows us to feel divinely rejected. The only thing we can possibly do is to wait for God's mercy—and when we least expect it, God can calm the storm with a single word.

—CASTLE

november 3

•

How do we respond to continuing days of spiritual anguish? We pray, but it feels as if we accomplish nothing. Neither solitude nor companionship is helpful. We become grouchy, unable to express in words what we are experiencing. We cannot end these torturous times by anything we do. We must endure them. Getting busy with charitable activity will help us to survive. Keep trusting the mercy of God who never fails anyone who has faith.

Even some of God's favors bring spiritual pain. The soul understands these are great kindnesses that exceed anything we deserve.

—CASTLE

november 4
·

Consider the ways God awakens the soul. Sometimes, when a person least expects it, His Majesty will awaken it in a flash. Although we hear no sound, the soul is thunderstruck with God's call.

O God, your sublime secrets are of a different character than the visible and audible things familiar to us. There are many questions I cannot answer. Comparisons are shallow, but I think it's like a spark leaping from a grill and striking the soul so that it feels a flaming fire. It never lasts. Sooner or later it burns out, leaving the soul longing for another spark.

—Castle

november 5
·

One way God can awaken a soul is with an inner voice. This "voice" comes in many ways and is difficult to define. Some seem to come through the ears, others from within the soul.

The inner voice I speak of can come from God, from the devil, or from one's own imagination. Don't think you are a better person because you sense this inner voice—even if it is genuinely from God. The only good that results is in how you respond to what you hear. If what you hear is not in agreement with the Scriptures, pay no attention to it at all.

—CASTLE

november 6

•

There are some clues that will help you to determine if God is the source. The first and best indication is in the *power and authority* of the voice. Things are better because you heard it. It makes a difference. Calmness replaces distress, for instance.

The second sign is *peaceful tranquility* in the soul combined with an eagerness to sing praises to God.

The third sign is that the *words stick in the memory* better than ordinary conversation. There is a strong faith in the truth of what you heard. Even if all the evidence indicates that the soul misunderstood, and much time passes, there is still confidence that God will find his own way to fulfill his promises.

Delays may cause doubts. The devil will actually prey upon your doubts. He will work hard to intimidate you if the inner voice spoke of something challenging that will bring honor to God. In spite of all these difficulties, there will remain a glowing ember of faith that God will overcome all obstacles and keep his word.

Now, if the inner voice is only the product of the imagination, none of these signs will be present. There will be no certainty, no peace, and no joy.

If what you think is an "inner voice" commands an action that will have dire consequences for yourself or for others, don't do anything until you have sought competent counseling.

—Castle

God can also unmistakably speak to the soul with a kind of intellectual vision that I'll describe later. This occurs in the depths of the soul. Only the soul has "ears" to hear it. The experience and the resulting behavior leave no doubt as to its authenticity. There is not a chance that you imagined it. One "hears" it with such clarity that every syllable and accent remains in memory. There is nothing dreamlike about it. Moreover, it does not spring from thoughts already in your mind. It comes without preparation. The words come with great understanding. The devil has no way of imitating these things.

Any soul that receives such favor and consolation from the Lord should be careful not to consider itself superior to other souls. The more it "hears," the more humble it should be. If humility does not follow, then distrust the source of the message.

If the Lord doesn't lead others along this path, they may think you could disregard what you "hear." This is impossible. We are not talking about imagined messages but gifts from God. The speaking spirit overwhelms all other thoughts, forcing the soul to pay attention. One cannot doubt there is a greater power than itself in charge of this castle. The result is deep devotion and humility. There is no cure for it.

God, let what I have tried to explain be helpful to others who have had similar experiences.

—CASTLE

november 8

The purpose of the trials and stresses one experiences is to increase your desire to enjoy being with the Spouse. His Majesty, understanding our weakness, is enabling the soul by allowing these difficulties to gain the courage to draw close to so great a Lord.

You laugh and think this sounds foolish because it doesn't take courage to be married to a king. Any woman would quickly agree to such an opportunity with an earthly king. But when it comes to the King of heaven, more courage is required than you think. We are naturally timid when we approach God, and if God did not give us courage, it would be impossible. God actually draws the enraptured soul out of its senses. Otherwise, it might die.

—CASTLE

november 9

.

I can't find a suitable illustration of what I'm discussing. None are accurate comparisons. I will try to explain it by asking you to imagine entering a room of an important person or a glittering treasury. The Duchess of Alba once took me into such a room. I was stunned and wondered how the sight of so many objects would ever be useful. I laugh as I write about it because the Lord is letting me use this experience to explain something to you.

Many objects filled that room, but I quickly forgot them when I exited. I could not report any detail of workmanship. All I can say is that I remember seeing all of it together. In the same way, when God grants this favor to the soul, it perceives a multitude of wonderful things. Later, the soul retains the impression of splendors, but it is not able to describe them. I can only say that rather than being an imaginary vision, it is an intellectual one. Since my education is limited, I am too ignorant to explain this.

—CASTLE

november 10

O God, have pity on this poor little butterfly that carries such a burden it cannot fly. Allow it to fulfill what it wants to do for your honor and glory. Take no regard of its lowliness or how little it deserves. You have the power to make an escape route through the sea for Israelite slaves in Egypt. Have no pity for this little butterfly. With your strength, it can endure many trials. Let others see your magnificence in a feminine and lowly creature, at whatever cost, in order that others will recognize that it is not hers and give you praise. She would give a thousand lives if only one soul were to praise you a little more because of her. She understands she deserves none of this.

I'm not sure why that spontaneous prayer spilled from my pen.

—CASTLE

november 11

•

False tears are not my personal problem. I am certainly not tender. My heart is so hard it distresses me. But when this inner fire grows warm, it distills even a hard heart.

You will be sure when God's fire within you generates your tears, because they result in peace rather than instability. The only good thing I can say about false tears is that they damage the body rather than the soul.

Be suspicious of any devotional tears you shed.

—CASTLE

november 12

•

Instead of trying to accomplish anything through spiritual feelings, put your hands hard to work and practice virtue. Give your attention to these things, letting God send you feelings of piety. True spirituality will irrigate dry soil and produce much fruit. The less we pay attention to our spiritual feelings, the more there will be. They are the rain that falls from heaven.

Any emotion that results from our effort to induce it inside of us will never compare with that given to us by God. We may exhaust ourselves digging a well and never uncover a mud puddle. The proper thing to do is to place ourselves humbly in God's presence and allow him to give us what he desires, either moisture or dryness. God knows what we need.

—Castle

november 13

·

Sometimes our Lord grants the soul a sense of euphoria and an odd prayer beyond understanding. I write about this now in case it may happen to you. I think it is a deep union of our faculties. The Lord leaves them free to experience the joy without comprehending what is happening. It is such a delight that you will want to share it with others so that they may join you in praising our Lord. Praise is the dominant impulse. You will want to organize festivals and feasts as the prodigal son's father did. There is a feeling of security and being at home.

Constraining your desire to tell others about this great happiness will be painful. When St. Francis was beaten and robbed, he ran through the fields shouting that he was heralding God. Friar Peter of Alcántara behaved in a similar manner. Anyone who heard him thought he was insane. What blessed madness!

—CASTLE

november 14

·

Some people want to remain in the Prayer of Quiet continually. They enjoy it and want to prolong the experience. I advise them not to immerse themselves in this kind of prayer all the time. A full life brings a variety of experiences. Prayer must leave time for other activity.

I am concerned about anyone who says this is a continual delight. Question yourself if this mistaken notion traps you. If absorption in prayer continues interminably, it can be extremely dangerous for your brain.

Even the most spiritual person needs to remain in touch with the world. I made the mistake of remaining absorbed in prayer, waiting for a return of the pleasure I had experienced. It didn't work. It wasn't possible for me to keep this up constantly. My mind would wander. My soul was like a bird flying around looking for somewhere to land. I was losing a lot of time and not getting anywhere in either virtue or prayer. I thought I was doing the right thing, but a servant of God discussed this with me, cautioning me. Then I saw I was wrong.

—CASTLE

november 15

The more we advance, the nearer we are to Jesus. He becomes our companion. We will notice changes in the manner of his loving communication with us. To keep you from being afraid, I will try to prepare you even though you may never experience these things.

It may happen when you least expect it. You will suddenly be aware that Christ, our Lord, is beside you. You will not see him.

I know someone who received this and other favors from God. She couldn't understand how she perceived the nearness of Jesus without actually seeing him. She had no doubt that it was Jesus, but the experience frightened her.

Deeply concerned, she told her confessor about it. He wanted to know how she could be certain it was the Lord if she didn't see anything. She replied that she could not explain it. She realized the vision helped her to live habitually thinking of God. It seemed as though God was always watching her and continually able to hear her prayers. She felt he was walking beside her, but there were no sensual indications of this.

—CASTLE

november 16

•

Now let's consider imaginative visions. The devil intrudes more into these than in the others I have mentioned. When they come from the Lord, they are advantageous because they work in harmony with our human nature.

Imagine you have a precious jewel that has healing value in a gold chest. You have never looked inside to see it, but you know it is there. Carrying it protects your health. It is a prized possession, even though you have never seen it, because it has cured some of your illnesses. If you dared to catch a glimpse of it, you could not. The owner sealed the reliquary. When he loaned it to you, he kept the key. If he wants you to see it, he will open it; if he wants the stone back, he will take it.

When it pleases our Lord to give more pleasure to a soul, he reveals himself clearly. You may see him as he was in the flesh, or as he is after his resurrection. The vision can be as brief as a flash of lightning, but it remains indelible.

—CASTLE

november 17

·

A "vision" or "image" should not be understood as a painting, but as alive. One cannot dwell on it any more than the eye can look at the sun. Its brilliance is not painful but more like an infused light or a sparkling diamond. The enraptured, lowly soul is frightened. Whereas the Lord's presence is lovely beyond description, and far beyond the limits of our imagination and intellect, extraordinary splendor and dignity accompany it. He clearly reveals that he is Lord of heaven and earth. It's not that way with the kings of this world. They are ordinary people you would not recognize as kings except for their trappings, or unless they inform you of their position.

O Lord, we are Christians, but we do not know you. How will we bear it if you sternly say to us, "You that are accursed, depart from me" (Matt. 25:41)?

—CASTLE

november 18

•

When you hear that God grants wonderful favors, I strongly urge you to resist praying for them or having any desire for them. Although this is a very good path to follow, humility will make you circumspect. Remind yourself that you do not deserve these things.

I believe God will never grant favors to anyone who desires them. Leave it to the Lord. The safest way is to yearn for only what God wants for you. God loves us and knows more than we do. Let's place ourselves in God's hands. This will never be a mistake.

—CASTLE

november 19

Walk in truth before God and others. Have no desire for human accolades. Give God the credit for what is his. Have a low regard for this world that lies, cheats, and will not last.

I think I have figured out why God loves the virtue of humility. It is because God is ultimate Truth. If we are humble we walk in truth. After all, we cannot claim for ourselves anything more than misery and nothingness. If we do not acknowledge this, we are dishonest.

—Castle

november 20

Do you think the little dove or butterfly is satisfied after it reaches the upper levels of the interior castle? Will it relax now and be content to die here?

No. Absolutely not. The little butterfly is more miserable here than when it was at the lower levels. Even though it may have received these elevated favors for many years, it lives with greater pain. Now that it has discovered a clearer view of the glory of God, realizing that it remains at a distance, its desire to be with the Lord increases each year.

Don't limit God, though. If God wants, he can bring someone to himself in a moment of our time.

—CASTLE

november 21
•

You may think that I have said so much about spiritual matters that nothing more could remain. But as God is infinite, so are his works. Who will ever tell of all his mercies and wonders? It can't be done.

Therefore, everything I have said, and will go on to say, in no way exhausts the possibilities of speaking about God.

—CASTLE

november 22

In the same way that God has a private place in heaven, he has a dwelling place in each human soul. It is here that a kind of spiritual marriage takes place between God and his spouse, the soul. In this union, God removes the blinding scales from our spiritual eyes and we see the Blessed Trinity with an intellectual vision. The soul sees what we believe by faith.

O God, help me! There is such a difference in hearing and believing these things and actually being able to perceive and understand the truth of them directly. In the deepest interior place we experience firsthand recognition.

—CASTLE

november 23

You must think that a person whom God permits to enter into the deepest part of the castle becomes so spiritually absorbed that it is impossible to attend to ordinary responsibilities. On the contrary, there is an intensification of service to God in the world.

The person I spoke of found herself greatly improved. Even though she had to deal with many problems and business details, it seemed to her that the essence of her soul remained in that interior room. Part of her soul suffered trials while the other part continued to enjoy peace and quiet with God. It was as though the Martha part complained about the Mary part.

This may seem foolish to you, but this is the way it actually happens even though no division affects the soul. There are many delicate issues in the interior that I am not bold enough to attempt to explain. We will see it all clearly in heaven. We will understand these secrets there.

—Castle

november 24

•

One day, when I had finished Communion, the resurrected Lord revealed himself in bright splendor, beauty, and majesty. He told me it was time that we had a mutual interest in each other's business. He said other things I understood but must not repeat.

This experience was frightening because it was so different from all the other divine encounters with which I was familiar. It was a powerful, intimate vision. It was a marriage, a union similar to melting two candles together so that they make one flame from one wick. It is like rain mixing with the water of a river—it is all water, inseparable. This must be what St. Paul means when he says, "Anyone united to the Lord becomes one spirit with him" (1 Cor. 6:17). He also says, "For to me, living is Christ and dying is gain" (Phil. 1:21). The soul can repeat these words because this is where the little moth dies joyfully. Christ has become its life.

—CASTLE

november 25

•

Now let's see how different this new life is. First of all, there is a total forgetting of self. It is as though the soul no longer has an independent existence. It thinks of nothing for itself and only desires to honor God. Additionally the soul has a new kind of willingness to suffer. Whatever His Majesty orders is acceptable and good. There is no fretting.

Persecution brings an inner joy. Hostility toward others is out of the question. One prays for one's enemies.

These effects are not constant in the soul. There is a natural shift within the castle from time to time. Sometimes our Lord leaves us exposed to the venomous snakes in the exterior rooms. The truth of the matter is that those who are nearest Christ are those who have the greatest trials. But if we look at the Crucified One, such difficulties become trifles. We do not pray for our own pleasure and entertainment, but to find the strength to serve God.

—CASTLE

november 26
•

The Lord brings the soul to its center where he lives. The heaven above the earth is always in motion, but this empyreal heaven where the Lord is does not move. There is stillness here. Our senses and imagination do not disturb our peace.

I don't mean to suggest that once God grants a soul this favor, it becomes confident of its salvation and never stumbles again. The soul is only secure as long as the divine

Majesty holds it in his hand. Even though this state may continue to exist for years, it lives in greater fear that it may offend God and has a strong urge to serve him. The soul is at peace, but war, struggles, and fatigue continue to plague us.

While the King is in his palace many troublesome things occur in his kingdom. Even while many creatures create disturbances in the other dwelling places of this interior castle, none of them cause trouble here at the center. Our passions are conquered.

I laugh at myself as I write these things. Such comparisons are not satisfactory, but I can't think of anything else. You may think as you please, but what I have said is true.

—CASTLE

november 27

•

Yes, there are rooms that are off limits unless the Lord of the castle invites you in. If you find any doors shut, pass them by. Do not try to force your way in. Aggressiveness angers him; humility pleases him. If you understand that you have no right to enter the third rooms, you will be drawn into the fifth. There you will be able to serve God in such a way that he may eventually bring you to his private dwelling place. Then, when you return, you will find the door always open to you. Learning how to enjoy this castle will allow you to be at peace even when God demands much of you in the world. You will know you can return to a castle that no one can take away from you.

There are also lovely gardens, fountains, and mazes. You will want to praise God for creating all of these things.

—CASTLE

november 28

•

When I was reading books about prayer, I did not have a spiritual director. I was trying to educate myself. I discovered that if our Lord hadn't shown me the way, I wouldn't have learned much from books. But I had no idea what I was doing.

When I began to discover the Prayer of Quiet, I tried to discard every earthly thought. It seemed presumptuous to me to think I might lift up my soul, but I thought I had a sense of the presence of God. I tried to recollect myself before him and found this method of prayer pleasurable. No one could possibly have convinced me to return to the contemplation of Christ's humanity.

Jesus Christ crucified! The memory of my mistaken judgment grieves me. It was an act of high treason and the product of ignorance. I have returned to my habit of delighting in our Lord, especially during Communion. I would like to have a picture of him always before my eyes because I have not engraved him as deeply in my soul as I wish.

—LIFE

november 29

Sometimes the Lord grants contemplation to an individual after only a year or so of practice. Another person may actively pray for twenty years and never experience it. God has reasons for this difference.

We think many years of study will teach us what we can only learn through personal experience. Many who want to be spiritual guides believe they can tell the difference in religious experiences even though they have little familiarity with such phenomena.

As long as a spiritual director has a good education, it should be possible to offer assistance to other souls. Let any director be careful and reasonable while dealing with inner and exterior concerns. Regarding someone's supernatural experiences, the director need only search for parallels in sacred Scripture.

—LIFE

november 30
.

Here is a summary of everything I am trying to teach you: completely surrender to God, place your personal desires in his hands, and detach yourself from material things. By now, you should recognize the importance of this. We are preparing to complete a journey and will soon be drinking from the fountain of living water. Unless we totally turn our personal wills over to God, allowing God to do what is best for us, he will not allow us to drink it.

We are helpless and cannot design any way around this. Pray, "Lord, if you think it's best to give me difficulties and trying circumstances, then give me strength and let them come. If persecution, illness, dishonor, and need have brought me to you, my Father, I will not turn away from you or from them. Give me your kingdom so that I may do your will because Christ asks this of me. I am yours. Do with me as you please."

—WAY

december

If we think of how much we owe our Lord, who he is and what we are, our souls will develop. When we set our own joy aside to do our work in the world, we give pleasure to God. Our Lord himself said, "Just as you did it to one of the least of these who are members of my family, you did it to me" (Matt. 25:40). He wants the loving soul to take the same path he did: "He humbled himself and became obedient to the point of death" (Phil. 2:8).

If we are distressed that we must turn aside from being absorbed in God, we likely are victims of a subtle self-love that doesn't permit us to see that we want to please ourselves rather than God. Anyone who truly loves God is not able to rest when so much of God's work is waiting for her attention. There is no way we can linger with delightful contemplation when God is clearly telling us to perform a job that is important.

Others pointed this out to me when my crowded schedule bothered me. I didn't want them to see me caught in stressful circumstances with so much business demanding most of my time. I mentioned that spiritual growth wasn't possible in a situation like mine. O Lord, you do things in ways we cannot imagine! When a soul is committed to loving you, you desire nothing other than that it obey and seek to do what you want it to do. There is no need for us to seek other paths. You, my Lord, guide us in the most beneficial way. Looking back, we are surprised to discover spiritual improvement even while attending to the details of business.

—FOUNDATIONS

december 2

·

When you give yourself up to God, you will no longer worry about food and flesh. You will fill your hours of prayer with more important concerns. You will have plenty of time to take care of life's necessities. There is no need to dwell on these details. Continue working in order to support yourself, but allow your soul to rest. Turn all of your concerns about having enough material blessings over to your Lord. He gladly accepts these burdens from you.

He will never fail you if you abandon yourself to God's will.

—WAY

december 3

·

Preachers and teachers are required to live in the world. They have no option of living a sheltered life. Their duty is to live among people and sometimes to outwardly behave in the same ways that they do. It isn't simple to be required to conduct business with the world while simultaneously existing in exile from it. They must be both men and angels.

These are not the days for imperfect teachers.

—WAY

december 4

My five years at St. Joseph's in Avila were the most restful years of my life. My soul continues to recall the serenity and silence there. I remember the arrival of some religious women entrapped by the well-dressed fashion of the world. But with a complete change of interests, they came to the Lord's house and were much more perfect than I. I was delighted to have such dedicated pure souls around me. Their only desire was to praise and serve God.

His Majesty provided for our needs without the necessity of begging, but on a few occasions when we ran short of supplies, these women seemed to enjoy it.

As the superior at St. Joseph's, I never worried about having the essentials. I knew the Lord would not ignore those who were dedicated to pleasing him. When we only had a little, I directed that we should give what we had to those with the greatest need. Each one decided what she could do without, and the food stayed in the pantry until God sent enough for all of us.

—FOUNDATIONS

december 5

Don't worry if you seem uncouth or if others say you are a hypocrite. Such critics will not bother to visit you and waste your time. They can't speak your language, making it necessary for you to translate everything you want to say into their language. What a bother! Experience has shown me that this effort drags one's spiritual life down. Along the road we travel, peace and quiet are of great value.

Now, if your visitors want to learn your spiritual language, it is not your job to teach them. Assure them they will benefit if they learn it themselves. Be gentle with them and pray for them. With your influence they will recognize its value and seek a master teacher.

—WAY

december 6

You may feel secure, certain that you will never regress and repeat old mistakes. You think you know everything there is to know about the errors we can make in this world.

You say, "I understand all this comes to an end. Anyway, I'm getting more pleasure now from being conscious of God."

This is a serious temptation all beginners face. The new Christians' false sense of security exposes them to repeated blunders. This becomes discouraging, and God has to work to keep us from slipping back further than we were before we committed ourselves to serious prayer.

Regardless of Christ's pledges of love, never become so confident that you let your guard down. Avoid every opportunity for sin.

—WAY

december 7

•

Consider what you are doing, Lord. You seem to be forgetting my great wickedness too quickly. My Creator, don't pour such valuable liquor into a broken bottle. You know I spill and fritter it away. Don't put your treasure in a place where it will not find proper respect.

You turn a city over to a mayor who is a coward. You give the fortress keys to one who quickly opens the door to the enemy. Your love for me, eternal King, is so great that you risk the care of precious jewels. You put them in the hands of one who is shameful, lowly, frail, miserable, and of no importance. She attempts to preserve them with your help, but she isn't able to use them to help anyone else. You have not only hidden but buried your treasure in dirt. You should grant these favors to someone more qualified to use them and increase them for your glory. I would gladly turn them over to such a person.

I used to say things like that. Now I understand my foolishness and lack of humility. The Lord knows exactly what is proper and that I would lack the strength for salvation if His Majesty did not shower me with so many favors.
—LIFE

december 8

The illness of Domingo Báñez distresses me. He probably did one of those customary Advent penances such as sleeping on the floor. It is unusual for him to be sick like this. Tell him to keep his feet covered. Pain is not difficult for him to endure, but it is a wretched thing for any of us that can last for many days.

Be sure he is wearing enough warm clothes. Bless God; he is doing a little better now. Pain like this, even when an enemy suffers it, always stirs me to pity. Give him my regards and best wishes.

—LETTER TO MARÍA BAUTISTA, 1576

december 9

.

I wish we five friends in Christ could get together secretly now and then. We could spot any pretenses we have and help each other to improve. We do not know ourselves as well as others know us. We would have to do this in secret because this kind of sharing is not popular today.

Even preachers are being careful to write sermons that don't offend anyone. They mean well, and they live decent lives. Why, then, do their sermons not result in anything positive? Why don't their listeners renounce their sins?

I think it is because the preachers are being too cautious. They are not on fire with God's love the way the apostles were. There is not much heat in their sermons. There is no way they could ever preach with the same passionate flames as the apostles, but I would like to see a little more enthusiasm. They would have it if they disregarded this world and its honors and did not care about gain or loss. Let them speak the truth for the glory of God.

—LIFE

december 10

•

I am confident, my Lord, in these servants of yours who are in this house. They have only one desire and work for only one thing. They want to please you. For your sake they have abandoned their slight possessions, wishing they could have given you more. You, my Creator, are grateful, and I am sure you will answer their prayers. When you were in the world, Lord, you did not despise women but always turned aside to help them, demonstrating great compassion. You found much faith and love in them.

—WAY

december 11

God's mercy and goodness are so great that even as we are busily engaged in worldly activities and pleasures he calls us continuously. He is eager for us to desire to be with him. This divine attraction is so sweet and strong that the poor soul grieves because it is not able to respond immediately.

God speaks to us through the comments of others. It may be while we're conversing with good people, or listening to a sermon, or reading books.

God also communicates with us through illness and difficult circumstances.

Even the feeblest prayer opens a way for God to speak with us. Don't despair. God will wait years for you, if he knows you have the desire.

—Castle

december 12

My padre, I nearly forgot to tell you: the woman bonesetter came to work on my arm. The prioress in Medina was very helpful in sending her. The cure turned out to be a genuine struggle both for her and for me. It has been a long time since I fell and broke it, and I could not use my wrist. The struggle caused terrible pain.

I endured the torture by thinking I could feel a little of what our Lord suffered. I rejoiced in this possibility and it seemed to help. I think the procedure was successful, but so much intense pain continues it is difficult to be sure. I am able to move my hand now and I can lift my arm as high as my head. It will certainly take time for everything to mend. If we had delayed having this done even a little longer, I would be a cripple, but if that is what God had wanted I would not be greatly upset.

I have suffered much since you left here, my padre. My flesh grows weary and my soul is fainthearted, but my will, I think, remains strong.

—LETTER TO JERÓNIMO GRACIÁN, 1578

december 13

If you decide to return something that God has given to you, dedicate it entirely to God. You will make a huge mistake if you act like those who lend something while expecting to get it back. You haven't given anything if you remain attached to it. Let it go.

If we have dedicated our brief lives to God, we should determine to keep the commitment, regardless of our struggles. This time is a gift to us; it is not our own. God may expect us to give an account for how we are using it.

Of course, we will need to turn aside briefly now and then to take care of earthly business. This doesn't mean misusing God's time. God pays no attention to such things as long as our dedication remains. But necessities that distract us from time to time are trivialities. If you dedicate these activities to God, they are acceptable as a gift. His judgment of us is generous rather than exacting. God readily forgives large debts.

—Way

december 14

Do not seek spiritual favors. Instead of complaining about a drought or pleading for consolations, take up the cross that Christ carried upon his shoulders. This cross is also for you to carry. Suffer with him and everything else will become less important.

You may think you will make better progress if God will only give you some encouragement, but His Majesty knows what we need. "You do not know what you are asking" (Matt. 20:22). Do not think that you must use fancy language or experiment in areas that are unknown to you. Everything necessary is in this spiritual harmony with God's will.

If you stumble along the way, do not be discouraged or stop trying. God will bring good even out of your fall.

—CASTLE

december 15

Once when I was praying, I felt Christ close by me. I didn't see him, but I knew he was with me. I had no idea this kind of vision was a possibility. I was extremely frightened and burst into tears. He reassured me with one word, and I recovered my poise. This was not an imaginary experience. I clearly perceived that he was at my right side.

I immediately reported this to my confessor. He wanted to know what Jesus looked like. I repeated that I had seen nothing.

"Then how did you know it was Christ?"

"I can't explain it, but I know he was close by my side." I fumbled around for comparisons, but there are no analogies available. I saw Christ neither with the eyes of the body nor with those of the soul. It was not an imaginary vision. It would be similar to a blind person sensing someone's nearness, but not exactly like that. None of the senses is involved, and yet the perception is clearer than the sun.

My confessor then asked me, "Who told you it was Jesus Christ?"

I replied, "He told me himself, but even before that I understood who he was." God can speak to the soul without speaking. There is too much of heaven in this language to make it understood on earth. The vision and the language are matters of pure spirituality.

—Life

december 16

•

It would require more time than I have to respond fully to your question about prayer. The short answer is that what you report is common for anyone who has reached contemplation. I have frequently mentioned this to you, but you don't remember. Seasons change during the year, and it's the same process in the interior life. There is no other way it can be. It's not your fault. Don't let it bother you.

I must disqualify myself as a judge because I have a conflict of interest. I am naturally inclined toward solitude, although I have had little of it. Since this is a feature of our order, I might advise for you what I would prefer for myself. Discuss your concern with Father Rector and he will know what to recommend for you. Try to determine the strongest impulse of your spirit. I am leaving you in God's hands because I am writing so many letters it is remarkable I have already said this much. The messenger is waiting.

—LETTER TO ANTONIO GAYTÁN, 1574

december 17

If it is possible to experience shame in heaven, I will be the most ashamed soul there. We will at least join the "Daughters of Jerusalem" (Lk. 23:28) in weeping for ourselves if we do not help Jesus carry his cross. What enjoyment can there be in the distractions of this life when we realize how much he paid?

Give up your riches for Christ and you will be rich. Seek no honor and you will become honored. You will be pleased when others think you are crazy. There are not many holy people regarded as mad today because they perform heroically as true lovers of Christ.

O world, world! You are gaining credit because few know what you are. We suppose God is pleased when people consider us wise and discreet. We think we need to go around with dour expressions in a dignified way in order to do any good. Religious persons who wear old and patched clothing puzzle us. It seems a novelty, and scandalous to the weak, if they give themselves to prayer. The world has forgotten religious perfection and the grand recklessness of the saints.

Our reserve causes more harm in these troubled times than any discomfort a spiritual person may cause with words and demonstrations. Our Lord obtains much fruit when holding the world in contempt is scandalous. We need to exhibit something similar to what our Lord and his apostles endured, and we need it now more than ever.

—LIFE

december 18

A great servant of God, with good intentions, advised us to turn our monastery business over to others. This caused a lot of trouble that was difficult to untangle. I can't state briefly everything that happened between the beginning and the completion of the monastery—but the first six months and the last six months were the most painful.

When things in Avila calmed down, the Lord sent us a Dominican friar who worked skillfully on our behalf. He told me he had no reason to come but had heard of our problems as if by chance. He convinced the authorities to let me enter this house with some nuns from the monastery of the Incarnation.

Our singing stirred great devotion among those present. Our greatest persecutors became great benefactors. Then they approved what they had previously condemned. They gradually withdrew from the lawsuit and considered what we had accomplished in the face of so much opposition to be a work of God. Today no one thinks we should not have founded St. Joseph's. The Lord moves them to give us alms without any begging on our part. We have everything we need, and I trust our Lord for the future.

I am pleased to live among these detached nuns. We enjoy solitude and don't encourage visitors unless they help us kindle more love for the Bridegroom. The only thing we talk about is God. We keep the rule of Our Lady of Carmel given in 1248. It's somewhat severe. We don't eat meat except when necessary; we fast eight months of the year and practice other austerities according to the primitive rule. Still, the sisters think the rule is light on many points and have tightened our observances.

Whoever relaxes this rule that we have no difficulty keeping will do something very wrong. We arranged this for those who desire to be alone with Christ. Thirteen is the maximum number of nuns permitted here. I am sure this is the right number. We have few troubles and excellent health. Joy and cheerfulness prevail. If anyone considers our rule hard, let her blame herself and not the rule of the house. Delicate persons who are not saints can bear it all gracefully because they have the true spirit. Let others go to another monastery where they may work out their salvation in the way they prefer.

—LIFE

december 19

The evolution of my prayers amazes me. If I want to pray for something I know our Lord does not desire, I can't do it. If I try to pray for it anyway, it is a weak prayer with little spirit. I'm not able to pray more forcefully even if I want. On the other hand, if I pray for something God intends to grant, I can do this constantly and with much enthusiasm. Such prayers are spontaneous and irresistible.

There is a great difference between these two kinds of prayer, and it's difficult for me to explain. When I try to ask God for something that is not his will, even though it may be important to me, I'm tongue-tied. I can't get it out. In the second case, I speak clearly and intelligibly to someone who seems to be a willing listener. The first case reminds me of vocal prayer. The second is more like a prayer of contemplation.

I prefer a brief prayer that promptly produces impressive results. For me, this would be better than a prayer that continues for years but never results in a resolution to do anything for God other than some trifling service. Such results from prayer are like a grain of salt, without weight or bulk, which a bird might carry off in its beak. We imagine these pitiable efforts are something fine.

True, God values even the poorest effort we make for him. I only mean to say that I don't make a big deal out of my work on his behalf.

—LIFE

december 20

Sometimes my soul is subject to a kind of silly foolishness. I am doing neither good nor evil, but simply drifting along with others without pain or pleasure and indifferent to life and death. My soul is like a little donkey, grazing and thriving on food another gives it without giving it a thought. It bears its humble life patiently, but it's not really going anywhere. This is like sailing with a gentle wind, unconscious of forward motion.

At other times the effects are impressive. The soul can feel itself growing, and insatiable desires burst into flame. This reminds me of little springs I have seen flowing out of the ground, constantly stirring sand and pebbles. This truly describes souls in this state. Their love remains active; unable to constrain themselves, they always reach upward. Love thoroughly saturates the soul and it cannot contain itself. It wants others to drink because there is more than enough.

I can't forget that living water our Lord mentioned to the Samaritan woman. It has a great attraction for me. When I was a little child, even though I didn't understand it the way I do today, I frequently asked our Lord for that living water. I had a picture of it captioned, "Sir, give me this water" (Jn. 4:15).

This love is like a great fire, constantly needing fuel. I am content to bring a little straw to throw into it. Sometimes I laugh at myself; other times I grieve. I feel compelled to do something good for God's service, but I'm unable to do more than put some flowers on holy images, polish things, and adjust furniture in the chapel. I'm embarrassed to mention the trivial things I do. The small penances I perform require our Lord to accept my good intentions. It is all worthless, and I laugh at myself.

—LIFE

december 21

Make an effort to be pleasant around others. Try to get along as well as possible with those who conduct business with you. Let them enjoy talking with a religious person. Make your way of life attractive rather than repulsive to them. Set a good example by warmly encouraging and humoring those you meet.

God pays no attention to trivial things that sometimes bother us. Don't let them reduce your courage and blessings. Make every effort not to offend God, and don't let your soul live in seclusion.

With love and fear of God we can journey through life in quiet peace, never worrying about falling into a pit or failing to reach our destination. Life always comes with risks. When our Teacher ended his prayer, this is what he said to his heavenly Father: "Rescue us from the evil one" (Matt. 6:13).

—WAY

december 22

I exhausted my soul trying to live by religious and social rules. They told me to keep all my thoughts on God, but I also needed to remember etiquette. Living in a religious house does not excuse me from being polite. I must remember small details of status and honor. Monks and nuns should be above worldly customs, but we are required to be charming in constantly changing ways. I might put up with these niceties if I could learn them once and for all. Even addressing a letter is a chore. Conflicting rules call for blank space in one corner and then in another. An individual is addressed as "illustrious" one day and "magnificent" another.

There will be no end to changing protocol when dealing with this world's important people. I am not yet fifty and I have seen so much change I don't know how to live. I feel sorry for spiritual people who must live in the world. They carry a dreadful cross.

I'm talking foolishly. I have turned away from speaking of God's greatness to complain about the small-mindedness of the world. I am ready to leave it. Let someone else fret over these petty things. The next life will be unchanging. Amen.

—LIFE

december 23

.

This is an enjoyable time. May your soul's progress also be a pleasure. Attend confession as a preparation for Christmas and pray for me.

No matter how much I try, God doesn't allow me to be poor. In a way this makes me unhappy, but it certainly makes it easier to pay our bills. I am thinking of small things I bought for you, how much I paid for them, and the balance available for the larger expenses of the order. I carefully maintain an accounting of what I spend. Unless I have extra money, there is no way I can spend anything other than what we use for the Incarnation monastery in Avila. Rather than purchase what I may desire, I spend it for greater service to God.

May His Majesty be our guide, grant you holiness, and give you a happy Christmas.

—LETTER TO JUANA DE AHUMADA, 1569

december 24

$\cdot$

Jesus be with you. You live so far from me, it seems as though you are in another world. I have been in poor health almost from the day of my arrival here at Avila. The reason I have not written is that I did not want to report this. Before Christmas I had a sore throat with fever. Doctors bled and purged me twice. I've suffered a malarial fever that recurs every fourth day since before Epiphany. I haven't been nauseated, and on the three days between the fevers I have been able to attend choir with the others and sometimes accompany them to meals. I don't expect the fevers to last much longer. Already I can see things improving in the house, and I try to get out of bed whenever the night-long fever breaks. Chills come about two in the morning, but they're bearable. Things are going well. With so many responsibilities and community struggles, it is amazing that I am able to continue. The greatest burden is letter writing. I have written four messages to the West Indies because the fleet is ready to sail.

—LETTER TO JUANA DE AHUMADA, 1572

december 25

Ah, shepherds who watch,
As you guard your flocks,
Here is a lamb for you,
Son of our Sovereign God.

He is poor and despised,
Add him to your guarded flock,
That a wolf may not take him
Without rejoicing in him.
Give me your shepherd's crook
That I may hold it in my hand,
Nothing will steal this Lamb.
Don't you see? He is Sovereign God.

You may think I am confused
By a combination of joy and sorrow.
If God is born today,
How then may he die?
Because he is also human.
Life is in his hands.
See what is in this Lamb.
Son of our Sovereign God.

—From "Al Nacimiento de Jesús"

december 26

I am eager to receive a report about your Christmas experience. You and your household have been on my mind this year even more than during previous Christmas seasons. I recommend all of you to our Lord and grieve because of your trials. Blessed is the one who came into our world for no other reason than to suffer. If we follow his example of suffering and keep his commandments, we will share his glory.

I wish I were near enough to visit you. On the feast of the Holy Innocents, I traveled from Valladolid through bitter winter weather to Palencia. Although I have my familiar ailments, the trip did not make anything worse.

Two days after I arrived here, I put up the bell at night and formally founded St. Joseph's Monastery. Amazingly, the people here are very happy about it. This may be because they love their bishop and know he supports us. Things are proceeding so well here that I trust in God this will become one of our best houses.

—LETTER TO JUANA DE AHUMADA, 1581

december 27

·

I am well now, but during the days before Christmas I became exhausted because of so much business that needed my attention. Even though I didn't feel well, I kept the Advent observance. Pass my regards around to others. Ask Padre Antonio de Jesús if he made a vow not to answer my letters.

I am pleased you have enough to make the annual payment on your monastery debt. God will provide all you need. May God watch over you.

This is the feast day of St. John the Evangelist.

—Letter to María de San José, 1576

december 28

·

I laughed aloud when I read your letter telling me you would express your thoughts about certain topics later. They handed your message to me on the last day of the Christmas feasts. Until now I could find no one who could carry a reply to you.

Someone instructed me to select a house and remain a permanent resident. The Council of Trent declares that I am to make no more foundations. I prefer not to become involved in the turmoil of reform, but the Lord keeps me entangled. Padre Gracián says I may relocate this summer since they won't need me here any longer. This venue has been good for my health and also for being quiet. Others here don't have an exaggerated opinion of me the way they do up there. But I still prefer to return.

I trust the Lord in these matters. I'll be content wherever I go.

—LETTER TO MARÍA BAUTISTA, 1575

december 29

•

My conclusions may be mistaken because they come from personal experience. I must not measure others against myself. Each individual is distinctive. When ordered to write about what happened to me, this is what I do. If the person reading this does not approve, he may destroy it. He knows best. I hereby grant him permission to publish what I have written about my miserable life while I'm still alive. Then I can't deceive others who might think there is something good in me.

What I write from this point on should remain our secret. If you should publish it, do not identify me as the author. I never mention myself by name and desire to maintain my privacy. If the Lord has allowed me to write anything worthwhile, it is not mine at all. I trust your scholarly judgment.

I am not an educated person and I have not lived a good life. The only person who knows anything about this project is the one who ordered me to write it. I have had no guidance and I almost have to steal time to work on it. We are a poor monastery and I should be spinning flax instead of writing.

If the Lord had given me larger mental capacity and a better memory, I may have derived some benefit from my reading and listening. If I have said anything correctly, it is because the Lord made it happen. Errors are my own fault and you can strike them out. Please respect my wishes. I have expressed things too freely.

—LIFE

december 30

Glory to God, I no longer worry about people's opinions. Many speak against me with the best of intentions. Some hesitate to speak with me or to hear my confession. My work to provide help for many souls receives misdirected criticism. I don't care. Maybe His Majesty put me in this little out-of-the-way corner with its strict enclosure (where I might as well be dead) in order to take me out of sight. The public has not forgotten me as much as I wish. I must continue to speak with some people, but I am in a secure haven. I am out of the world with a few holy companions. From this height, the things people may say or know about me make little difference. I give my attention to spiritual matters.

My life has become a kind of sleep, and my daily experience is dreamlike. I have no sense of pleasure or pain. When either occurs, the feeling quickly passes, as though waking from a dream.

I hope what I have written may be helpful to you. Little time remains for me, making it difficult for me to write, but the trouble will be worth it if I have said anything that will result in an act of praise to our Lord.

—LIFE

december 31

I will remember your soul before our Lord as long as I live.

Please grant me the favor of fervently serving God. From what I've written here, you can perceive what a good thing it is to occupy yourself completely with God as you have begun to do.

Bless God forever! I pray that, in his mercy, you and I will see each other in a place where we will be able to see more clearly the great things he has done for us and sing his praise forever. Amen.

—Letter to García de Toledo, 1562

about paraclete press

Who We Are

Paraclete Press is a publisher of books, recordings, and DVDs on Christian spirituality. Our publishing represents a full expression of Christian belief and practice—from Catholic to Evangelical, from Protestant to Orthodox.

We are the publishing arm of the Community of Jesus, an ecumenical monastic community in the Benedictine tradition. As such, we are uniquely positioned in the marketplace without connection to a large corporation and with informal relationships to many branches and denominations of faith.

What We Are Doing
Books

Paraclete publishes books that show the richness and depth of what it means to be Christian. Although Benedictine spirituality is at the heart of all that we do, we publish books that reflect the Christian experience across many cultures, time periods, and houses of worship. We publish books that nourish the vibrant life of the church and its people—books about spiritual practice, formation, history, ideas, and customs.

We have several different series, including the best-selling Living Library, Paraclete Essentials and Paraclete Giants series of classic texts in contemporary English; Voices from the Monastery—men and women monastics writing about living a spiritual life today; award-winning literary faith fiction and poetry; and the Active Prayer Series that brings creativity and liveliness to any life of prayer.

Recordings

From Gregorian chant to contemporary American choral works, our music recordings celebrate sacred choral music through the centuries. Paraclete distributes the recordings of the internationally acclaimed choir Gloriæ Dei Cantores, praised for their "rapt and fathomless spiritual intensity" by American Record Guide, and the Gloriæ Dei Cantores Schola, which specializes in the study and performance of Gregorian chant. Paraclete is also the exclusive North American distributor of the recordings of the Monastic Choir of St. Peter's Abbey in Solesmes, France, long considered to be a leading authority on Gregorian chant.

Videos

Our videos offer spiritual help, healing, and biblical guidance for life issues: grief and loss, marriage, forgiveness, anger management, facing death, and spiritual formation.

Learn more about us at our website: www.paracletepress.com, or call us toll-free at 1-800-451-5006.

SCAN
TO
READ
MORE

You may also be interested in . . .

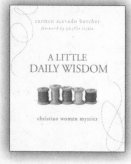

Little Daily Wisdom
Women Christian Mystics
Carmen Acevedo Butcher

ISBN: 978-1-55725-586-0, $16.99, TRADE PAPERBACK

Discover the strength, wisdom, and joyful faith of Christianity's legendary women—the medieval mystics. Their honesty and deep love for God will encourage and empower you every day of the year. This book of daily readings will help you create quiet space for focusing on God's love in the midst of a busy life. As you spend time with these great women, you will discover an astonishing view of a God who is tender, nurturing, forgiving, and as close as breath.

A Little Daily Wisdom
Joel Fotinos and August Gold

ISBN 978-1-55725-648-5, $14.99, TRADE PAPERBACK

365 inspiring Bible verses, designed to bring a life of faith and hope, to live a life confident in God's love. Not only do these daily verses give us strength in the moment, they are designed to be "bite-sized," so that they can be memorized easily. Once we memorize Bible verses, they are like "spiritual vitamins"—nourishment for our lives when we need them the most.